The Belgian Cookbook

Edited by Mrs Brian Luck

THE BELGIAN COOK-BOOK

EDITED BY

MRS. BRIAN LUCK

1915

"Lucullus, whom frugality could charm,
Ate roasted turnips at the Sabine Farm. "

PREFACE

The recipes in this little book have been sent by Belgian refugees from all parts of the United Kingdom, and it is through the kindness of these correspondents that I have been able to compile it. It is thought, also, that British cooking may benefit by the study of Belgian dishes.

The perfect cook, like Mrs. 'Arris or the fourth dimension, is often heard of, but never actually found, so this small manual is offered for the use of the work-a-day and inexperienced mistress and maid. It is not written in the interests of millionaires. The recipes are simple, and most inexpensive, rather for persons of moderate means than for those who can follow the famous directions for a certain savory: "Take a leg of mutton, " etc. A shelf of provisions should be valued, like love-making, not only for itself but for what it may become.

SAVORIES: If you serve these, let them be, like an ankle, small and neat and alluring. This dish is not obligatory; recollect that it is but a culinary work of supererogation.

SOUP: Let your soup be extremely hot; do not let it be like the Laodiceans. You know what St. John said about them, and you would be sorry to think of your soup sharing the fate which he describes with such saintly verve. Be sure that your soup has a good foundation, and avoid the Italian method of making *consommé*, which is to put a pot of water on to warm and to drive a cow past the door.

FISH: It is a truism to say that fish should be absolutely fresh, yet only too many cooks think, during the week-end, that fish is like the manna of the Hebrews, which was imbued with Sabbatarian principles that kept it fresh from Saturday to Monday. I implore of you to think differently about fish. It is a most nourishing and strengthening food —other qualities it has, too, if one must believe the anecdote of the Sultan Saladin and the two anchorites.

MEAT: If your meat must be cooked in water, let it not boil but merely simmer; let the pot just whisper agreeably of a good dish to come. Do you know what an English tourist said, looking into a Moorish cooking-pot? "What have you got there? Mutton and rice? " "For the moment, Sidi, it is mutton and rice, " said the Moorish cook;

"but in two hours, inshallah, when the garlic has kissed the pot, it will be the most delicious comforter from Mecca to Casa Blanca." Simmer and season, then, your meats, and let the onion (if not garlic) just kiss the pot, even if you allow no further intimacy between them. Use bay-leaves, spices, herbs of all sorts, vinegar, cloves; and never forget pepper and salt.

Game is like Love, the best appreciated when it begins to go. Only experience will teach you, on blowing up the breast feathers of a pheasant, whether it ought to be cooked to-day or to-morrow. Men, as a rule, are very particular about the dressing of game, though they may not all be able to tell, like the Frenchman, upon which of her legs a partridge was in the habit of sitting. Game should be underdone rather than well done; it should never be without well-buttered toast underneath it to collect the gravy, and the knife to carve it with should be very, very sharp.

VEGETABLES: Nearly all these are at their best (like brunettes) just before they are fully matured. So says a great authority, and no doubt he is thinking of young peas and beans, lettuces and asparagus. Try to dress such things as potatoes, parsnips, cabbages, carrots, in other ways than simply boiled in water, for the water often removes the flavor and leaves the fiber. Do not let your vegetable-dishes remind your guests of Froissart's account of Scotchmen's food, which was "rubbed in a little water."

SWEETS: It is difficult to give any general directions for sweets. They should be made to look attractive, and they should be constantly varied. The same remarks apply to savories, which last ought always to be highly seasoned, whether hot or cold.

MADE DISHES are a great feature in this little book. I have tried to help those small households who cook, let us say, a leg of mutton on Sunday, and then see it meander through the week in various guises till it ends its days honorable as soup on the following Friday. Endeavor to hide from your husband that you are making that leg of mutton almost achieve eternal life. It is noticeable that men are attracted to a house where there is good cooking, and the most unapproachable beings are rendered accessible by the pleasantness of a *soufflé*, or the aroma of a roast duck. You must have observed that a certain number of single men have their hearts very "wishful" towards their cook. Not infrequently they marry that cook; but it is less that she is a good and charming woman than that she is a good and charming cook. Ponder this, therefore; for I have known men otherwise happy, who long for a good beef-steak pudding as vainly as the Golden Ass longed for a meal of roses. Try these recipes, for really good rissoles and hashes. Twice-cooked meat can always be alleviated by mushrooms or tomatoes. Remember that the discovery of a new dish is of more use than the discovery of a new star, — besides which, you will get much more praise for it. And if on Wednesday you find that you have to eat the same part of the very same animal that you had on Monday, do not, pray, become exasperated; treat it affectionately, as I treat my black hat, which becomes more ravishing every time that I alter it. Only, do not buy extravagant make-weight for a scrap of cold meat that would be best used in a mince patty, or you will be like a man keeping a horse in order to grow mushrooms.

And, lastly, the good cook must learn about food what every sensible woman learns about love—how best to utilize the cold remains.

M. LUCK.

PART I

CAULIFLOWER SOUP

After you have boiled a cauliflower, it is a great extravagance to throw away the liquor; it is delicately flavored and forms the basis of a good soup. Wash well your cauliflower, taking great care to remove all grit and insects. Place it to simmer with its head downwards, in salted water; and, when it is tender, remove it. Now for the soup. Let all the outer leaves and odd bits simmer well, then pass them through a sieve. Fry some chopped onions, add the liquor of the cauliflower and the pieces that have been rubbed through the sieve, add a little white pepper and a slice of brown bread. Let all cook gently for half-an-hour, then, just before serving it, take out the slice of bread and sprinkle in two teaspoonfuls of grated Gruyere cheese.

FISH SOUP

When you buy fish and have it filleted, ask for the bones and trimmings to be sent also. Put a quart of milk to heat and add to it a bunch of mixed herbs, a few minced shallots, parsley, pepper and salt. Throw in your fish and cook for an hour. If you have any celery put in a piece, or two or three white artichokes. Strain the soup, taste it, and add more salt or more milk as you think necessary. Return to the pan. Take the yolk of an egg and just before taking the soup from the fire, stir it quickly in. This soup must never boil. It should be made out of the very white fish, excluding herring and mackerel.

STARVATION SOUP

If you have a pork-bone from the fresh meat, let it boil in water for an hour. Put the pan to cool and take off the fat, and remove the bone. Replace the pan on the fire and throw into it two pounds of Brussels sprouts. Do not add onions to this soup but leeks, and the hearts of cabbage. Pepper and spice to taste. Rub it through a sieve and let it be thick enough to form a thin purée.

IMMEDIATE SOUP, OR TEN MINUTES SOUP

Into a quart of boiling water throw two tablespoonfuls of either semolina or tapioca: let it boil for eight minutes with a dust of salt and pepper. Meanwhile, take your tureen, put quickly into it two yolks of very fresh eggs, add two pats of butter and two small spoonfuls of water to mix it. Stir quickly with the spoon, and when the soup has done its eight minutes' boiling, pour it on the egg and butter in the tureen. This is an extremely good soup. It is rendered still better by a small quantity of Bovril.

CHERVIL SOUP

Put a bone of veal on to cook in water, with four or five potatoes, according to the quantity desired. When these are tender, pass them through the tammy and return them to the soup. Chop up the chervil, adding to it half a dessert-spoonful of cornflour. Quarter of an hour before serving, put in the chervil, but take the cover off the pot, so that it remains a good green color. Pepper and salt to be added also.

[*V. Verachtert, Café Appelmans, Anvers.*]

A GOOD PEA SOUP

Soak your dried peas over-night. The following day boil some fresh water, and throw in the peas, adding a few chopped onions and leeks, with pepper and salt. Let the soup simmer for three hours on the top of the stove, giving it a stir now and then. If you have a ham-bone, that is a great improvement, or the water in which some bacon has been boiled is a good foundation for the soup, instead of the fresh water.

[*Mdlle. M. Schmidt.*]

WATERZOEI

This is an essentially Flemish soup. One uses carp, eels, tench, roach, perches, barbel, for the real waterzoei is always made of different kinds of fish. Take two pounds of fish, cut off the heads and tails, which you will fry lightly in butter, adding to make the sauce a mixed carrot and onion, three cloves, a pinch of white pepper, a sprig of parsley, one of thyme, a bay-leaf; pour in two-thirds of water and one-third of white wine till it more than covers the ingredients and let it simmer for half- an-hour. Then the pieces of fish must be cut an equal size, and they are placed to cook quickly in this liquor for twenty minutes. Five minutes before serving add a lemon peeled and cut into slices and the pips removed. Some people bind the sauce with breadcrumbs grated and browned. You serve, with this dish, very thin slices of bread and butter. For English tastes, the heads and tails should be removed when dressing the dish.

A GOOD BELGIAN SOUP

is called *crème de sauté*. Itself one of the most wholesome of vegetables, watercress combines admirably with potatoes in making soup. Wash, dry, and chop finely four ounces of the leaves picked from the stalks, fry slowly for five minutes with or without a thinly-sliced onion, add one pound of potatoes cut in small dice, and fry, still very slowly, without browning; pour in one quart of water or thin stock, simmer gently, closely-covered, for from thirty-five to fifty minutes, rub through a hair sieve, and having returned the puree to the saucepan with a half-teaspoonful of castor sugar, and salt and cayenne to taste, thicken with one table-spoonful of flour stirred smoothly into one breakfast-cupful of cold milk; boil up sharply, and serve sprinkled with watercress.

[*E. Haig.*]

BELGIAN PURÉE

Cook two pounds of Brussels sprouts in boiling water. Take them out, drain them and toss them in butter for five minutes, sprinkle them with a teaspoonful of flour, and then cook them in gravy (or meat extract and water), fast boiling, over a good fire, and keep the lid of the saucepan off so that they may remain green. Pass them through the sieve, leave them in ten minutes, bind the mixture with the yolks of three eggs, a pint of milk; then at the last minute one dessert-spoonful of butter for each pint and a half of soup.

AMBASSADOR SOUP

A pint and a half of either fresh peas, or of dried peas that have been soaked for six hours in cold water; a leek, and three onions chopped finely. Simmer till the peas are tender, then pass all through the sieve. Well wash some sorrel and chop it, and add as much as will be to your taste. In another pan cook five tablespoonfuls of rice, and add that to your soup. Simmer up again, stirring it all very well. This soup should be of a green color.

[*Mme. Georges Goffaux.*]

CRECY SOUP (BELGIAN RECIPE)

Take ten carrots, two onions, one leek, five potatoes, and cook all gently in water, with salt and pepper; when they are tender, rub them through the sieve and serve it very hot.

[*G. Goffaux.*]

FLEMISH SOUP

To two pounds of washed and picked Brussels sprouts add ten potatoes, two onions, two leeks, salt, pepper. Cook all gently and pass through a sieve. Add at the last moment a sprinkle of chopped chervil.

[*G. Goffaux.*]

TOMATO PURÉE

Begin by cleaning four potatoes, two leeks, a celery, four carrots, three pounds of big tomatoes; well wash all these vegetables and cut them in dice, the tomatoes a little larger. Cook them all gently for an hour in nearly two pints of gravy, to which you have already added two thick slices of bread and a pinch of salt. Take care that your vegetables do not stick to the bottom of the pan. When all is well cooked, pass it through a fine tammy. Add more gravy, or water and meat juice; make it of the consistency that you wish. Bring it to the boil again over the fire, adding pepper and salt, and just before serving a bit of fresh butter also. It is a great improvement to add at the last minute the yolk of an egg, mixed in a little cold water, quickly stirred in when the soup is off the fire.

The three recipes for seven or eight persons.

[*G. Kerckaert.*]

ONION SOUP

Mince some thick onions, five or six, and let them color over the fire in butter. Add a dessert-spoonful of flour, sprinkling it in, and the same amount in gravy; thicken it with potatoes and when these are cooked, peas, all through a sieve. Bring the purée to the right consistency with milk, and let it simmer for a few minutes before serving, adding pepper and salt.

[Gabrielle Janssens.]

POTAGE LEMAN

Make a good gravy with one and one-half pounds of skirt of beef. With one half of the gravy make a very good purée of peas—if possible the green peas—with the other half make a good purée of tomatoes. Combine the two purées, adding pepper and salt and a dust of cayenne. For each guest add to the soup a teaspoonful of Madeira wine, beat it all well and serve quickly. Or add, instead of Madeira, one dessert-spoonful of sherry wine.

This celebrated soup is honored by the name of the glorious defender of Namur.

[Gabrielle Janssens.]

TOMATO SOUP

Boil together six medium potatoes, a celery, two leeks, two carrots, and a pound of fresh tomatoes, with pepper, salt and a leaf of bay. Pass all through the sieve. Fry two or three chopped onions in some butter and add the soup to them. Boil up again for twenty minutes before serving. If you have no fresh tomatoes, the tinned ones can be used, removing the skin, at the same time that you add the fried onions.

[Mme. van Praet.]

SOUP, CREAM OF ASPARAGUS

Boil some potatoes and pass them through the sieve, add the asparagus- tops, with a pat of butter for each four tops; thin the soup with extract of meat and water, and at the last moment stir in the raw yolks of two eggs, and a little chopped parsley.

[Mme. van Praet.]

GREEN PEA SOUP

Put half a pound of dry green peas to soak overnight in water, with a teaspoonful of bicarbonate of soda in it. In the morning take out the peas and put them on the fire in about three-and-a-half pints of water. When the peas are nearly cooked, add five big potatoes. When all is cooked enough for the skins to come off easily, rub all through a sieve. Fry in some butter four or five onions and five or six leeks till they are brown, or, failing butter, use some fat of beef; add these to the peas and boil together a good half-hour. If possible, add a pig's trotter cut into four, which makes the soup most excellent. When ready to serve, remove the four pieces of trotter. Little dice of fried bread should be handed with the soup.

[*V. Verachtert.*]

VEGETABLE SOUP

Fry four onions till they are brown. Add them to three pints of water, with four carrots, a slice of white crumb of bread, five potatoes, a celery and a bunch of parsley, which you must take out before passing the soup through the sieve. A few tomatoes make the soup better; if they are tinned, do not add them till after the soup has been passed through the tammy; if they are fresh, put them in with the other vegetables. Simmer for an hour, add pepper and salt before serving.

[*V. Verachtert.*]

MUSHROOM CREAM SOUP

On a good white stock foundation, for which you have used milk and a bone of veal, sprinkle in some ground rice till it thickens, stirring it well for twenty minutes. Wash and chop your mushrooms, and fry them in butter. Add the yolk of an egg and bind it. This is a delicious soup.

[*Mme. van Marcke de Lunessen.*]

THE SOLDIER'S VEGETABLE SOUP

(Eight to ten persons)

Peel three pounds of vegetables. Put them in a large pot with all the vegetables that you can find, according to the season. In the winter you will take four celeries, four leeks, two turnips, a cabbage, two onions, pepper and salt, two-penny-worth of bones, and about five and one-half quarts of water. Let it all boil for three hours, taking care to add water so as to keep the quantity at five quarts. Rub all the vegetables through a tammy, crushing them well, and then let them boil up again for at least another hour. The time allotted for the first and second cooking is of the greatest importance.

LEEK SOUP

Cut up two onions and fry them till they are brown; you need not use butter, clarified fat will do very well. Clean your leeks, washing them well; cut them in pieces and fry them also; add any other vegetables that you have, two medium-sized potatoes, pepper, salt, and a little water. Let all simmer for three hours, and pass it through a fine sieve. Let there be more leeks than other vegetables, so that their flavor predominates.

[*Mme. Jules Segers.*]

CELERIS AU LARD

Take one pound of celery, cut off the green tops, cut the stems into pieces two-thirds of an inch long; put into boiling salted water, and cook till tender. Take one-half pound potatoes, peel and slice, and add to the celery, so that both will be cooked at the same moment. Strain and place on a flat fire-proof dish. Prepare some fat slices of bacon, toast them till crisp in the oven; pour the melted bacon-fat over the celery and potato, adding a dash of vinegar, and place the rashers on top. Serve hot.

Leeks may be prepared in the same way.

CABBAGE WITH SAUSAGES

Cut a large cabbage in two, slice and wash, put it into boiling water with salt, and when partly cooked, add some potatoes cut into smallish pieces. Cook all together for about an hour; then drain. Put some fat in a saucepan, slice an onion, brown it in the fat, add the cabbage and potato, and stew all together for ten minutes; then dish. Bake some sausages in the oven and dish them round the cabbage; serve hot.

Another way (easier)

Stew the cabbages, potato and sausages all together and dish up neatly.

LEEKS À LIEGOISE Take enough of leeks to make the size of dish required; if they are very thick, cut in two lengthwise; cut off the green tops; leaving only the blanched piece of stalk; put them into boiling salted water and cook thoroughly about one hour: strain and dish neatly on a fish-drainer. Have ready some hard-boiled eggs; shell them, cut in two, and place round the leeks; serve hot with melted butter, or cold with mayonnaise sauce.

N. B. The water in which the leeks have been boiled makes a wholesome drink when cold, or a nourishing basis for a vegetable soup.

[*From Belgians at Dollarfield, N.B.*]

A SALAD OF TOMATOES

To make a tomato salad you must not slice the fruit in a dish and then pour on it a little vinegar and then a little oil; that is not salad — that is ignorance.

Take some red tomatoes, and, if you can procure them, some golden ones also. Plunge each for a moment in boiling water, peel off the skin, but carefully, so as not to cut through the flesh with the juice. Take some raw onion cut in slices; if you do not like the strong taste, use shallot; and lay four or five flat slices on the bottom of the salad dish. Put the tomato slices over them, sprinkle with salt and just a dust of castor sugar. In four hours lift the tomatoes and remove the onions altogether. Make in a cup the following sauce: Dissolve a salt-spoonful of salt in a teaspoonful of tarragon vinegar. Stir in a dessert-spoonful of oil, dropping it slowly in, add a very little mustard, some pepper and a sprinkle of chopped chervil. Some people like chopped chives. Pour this over the tomato salad and leave it for an hour at least before serving it.

POTATOES AND CHEESE

Every one likes this nourishing dish, and it is a cheap one. Peel some potatoes and cut them in rounds. In a fireproof dish put a layer of these, sprinkle them with flour, grated cheese, pepper, salt, a few pats of butter. Then some more potatoes, and so on till the dish is full. Beat the yolks of two eggs in a pint of milk, add pepper and salt and pour it over the dish. Leave it on the top of the stove for five minutes, then cook it for half-an-hour in a moderate oven. Less time may be required if the dish is small, but the potatoes must be thoroughly cooked. The original recipe directs Gruyère cheese, but red or pale Canadian Cheddar could be used.

FRIDAY'S FEAST

Cook a medium cabbage till it is tender, and all the better if you can cook it in some soup. When tender, mince it and rub it through a sieve. Boil at the same time three pounds of chestnuts, skin them, keep ten whole, and rub the others through the sieve, adding a little milk to make a purée. Mix the purée with the cabbage, adding salt, pepper, and a lump of butter the size of a chestnut. Press it into a mold and cook it in a double saucepan for quarter of an hour. Take it out and decorate with the whole chestnuts.

RED CABBAGE

Take half a red cabbage of medium size, chop it very finely and put it in a pan; add a little water, salt, and pepper, three or four potatoes cut in fine slices and five lumps of sugar. Let it all simmer for two hours with the lid on. Then take off the cover and let it reduce. Before serving it, add either a bit of fat pork or some gravy, with a dessert- spoonful of vinegar. Stir it well before sending it to table.

[*Mrs. Emelie Jones.*]

ASPARAGUS À L'ANVERS

Clean a bunch of asparagus and cook it in salt water for fifteen minutes. To do this successfully, tie the bunch round with some tape and place it upright in a pan of boiling water. Let the heads be above the water so that they will get cooked by the steam and will not be broken. Simmer in this way to prevent them moving much. Meanwhile, hard-boil three eggs and chop some parsley. Lay the asparagus on a dish and sprinkle parsley over it, place round the sides the eggs cut in halves long-ways, and serve as well a sauce-boat of melted butter.

[*Mrs. Emelie Jones.*]

COOKED LETTUCE

Very often you will find that you cannot use all your lettuces, that they have begun to bolt and are no good for salad. This is the moment to cook them. Discard any bad leaves and wash the others carefully. Boil them for twelve minutes, take them off the fire, drain them and dry them in a clean cloth so as to get rid of all the water. Mince them finely, then put them into a saucepan with a lump of butter, pepper and salt. Stir till they begin to turn color, then put in a thimbleful of flour melted in milk. Stir constantly, and if the vegetable becomes dry, moisten with more flour and milk. Let it simmer for quarter of an hour, and turn it out as a vegetable with meat.

STUFFED CAULIFLOWER

Pick over a fine cauliflower, and plunge it for a moment in boiling water. Look over it well again and remove any grit or insects. Put it head downwards in a pan when you have already placed a good slice of fat bacon at the bottom and sides. In the holes between the pan and the vegetable put a stuffing of minced meat, with breadcrumbs, yolks of eggs, mushrooms, seasoning of the usual kinds, in fact, a good forcemeat. Press this well in, and pour over it a thin gravy. Let it cook gently, and when the gravy on the top has disappeared put a dish on the top of the saucepan, turn it upside down and slip the cauliflower out. Serve very hot.

GOURMANDS' MUSHROOMS

There was a man in Ghent who loved mushrooms, but he could only eat them done in this fashion. If you said, "Monsieur, will you have them tossed in butter?" he would roar out, "No—do you take me for a Prussian? Let me have them properly cooked."

Melt in a pan a lump of butter the size of a tangerine orange and squeeze on it the juice of half a lemon. The way to get a great deal of juice from a lemon is to plunge it first of all for a few minutes, say five minutes, in boiling water. When the butter simmers, throw in a pound of picked small mushrooms, stir them constantly, do not let them get black. Then in three or four minutes they are well impregnated with butter, and the chief difficulty of the dish is over. Put the saucepan further on the fire, let it boil for a few minutes. Take out the mushrooms, drain them, sprinkle them with flour, moisten them with gravy, season with salt and pepper, put them back in the butter and stir in the yolk of an egg. Add also a little of the lemon juice that remains. While you are doing this you must get another person to cut and toast some bread and to butter it. Pour on to the bread the mushrooms (which are fit for the greatest saints to eat on Fridays), and serve them very hot.

POMMES CHÂTEAU

Take twenty potatoes, turn them with a knife into olive shape, boil them in salted water for five minutes; drain them and put them on a baking-tin with salt and butter or dripping. Cook them in a very hot oven for thirty minutes, moving them about from time to time. Sprinkle on a little chopped parsley before serving.

CHIPPED POTATOES

Take some long-shaped potatoes, peel them and smooth them with the knife. Cut them into very thin rounds.

Heat the grease pretty hot, dry the slices of potato with a cloth, put them into the frying basket and plunge them into the fat. When they are colored, take the basket out, let the fat heat up again to a slightly higher temperature, and re-plunge the basket, so that the slices become quite crisp. Serve with coarse salt sprinkled over.

CHICORY À LA FERDINAND

Boil and chop in medium-sized pieces the chicory, mince up a few chives according to your taste and heat both the vegetables in some cream, adding salt and pepper. Pour on a dish and decorate with chopped hard- boiled eggs.

APPLES AND SAUSAGES

This dish comes from the French border of Belgium; it tastes better than you would think. Take a pound of beef sausages, and preferably use the small chipolata sausages. (What a delightful thing if the English would make other kinds of sausages as well as their beef and pork ones!) Fry then your sausages lightly in butter, look upon them as little beings for a few moments in purgatory before they are removed to heaven, among the apples. Keeping your sausages hot after they are fried, take a pound of brown pippin apples, pare them and core them. Cut them into neat rounds quarter of an inch thick, put them to cook in their liquor of the sausages (which you are keeping hot elsewhere), and add butter to moisten them. Let them simmer gently so as to keep their shape. Put the apple- rings in the center of the dish, place the sausages round them. This dish uses a good deal of butter, but you must not use anything else for frying.

STUFFED CHICORY

Make a mince of any cold white meat, such as veal, pork or chicken, and add to it some minced ham; sprinkle it with a thick white sauce. In the meantime the chicories should be cooking; tie each one round with a thread to keep them firm and boil them for ten minutes. When cooked, drain them well, open them lengthwise very carefully, and slip in a spoonful of the mince. Close them, keeping the leaves very neat, and, if necessary, tie them round again. Put them in a fire-proof dish with a lump of butter on each, and let them heat through. Serve them in their juice or with more of the white sauce, taking care to remove the threads.

[*Madame Limpens.*]

TOMATOES STUFFED WITH BEANS

Halve and empty the tomatoes, and put a few drops of vinegar in each. Cook your beans, whether French beans or haricots or flageolets, and stir them, when tender, into a good thick bechamel sauce. Let this get cold. Empty out the vinegar from the tomatoes and fill them with the mixture, pouring over the top some mayonnaise sauce and parsley.

[*Madame van Praet.*]

CABBAGE AND POTATOES

Boil the cabbages in salted water till tender. Chop them up. Brown an onion in butter, and add the cabbage, salt, pepper, and a little water. Slice some potatoes thickly, fry them, and serve the vegetable with cabbage in the center, and the fried potatoes laid round.

[*Mdlle. M. Schmidt, Antwerp.*]

SPINACH À LA BRACONNIÈRE

Cook two pounds of well-washed spinach; drain it, and pass it through a sieve; or, failing a sieve, chop it very finely with butter, pepper and salt. Do not add milk, but let it remain somewhat firm. Make a thick bechamel sauce, sufficient to take up a quarter of a pound of grated Gruyère, and, if you wish, stir in the yolk of a raw egg. Lay in a circular dish half a pound of minced ham, pour round it the thick white sauce, and round that again the hot spinach. This makes a pretty dish, and it is not costly.

[*Mme. Braconnière.*]

A DISH OF HARICOT BEANS

Put the haricots to soak for six hours in cold water. Boil them in water with one carrot, one onion, salt, two cloves, a good pinch of dried herbs. Drain off the liquor from the haricots. Chop up a shallot, and fry it in butter; add your haricots, with pepper and salt and tomato purée. Stir well, and serve with minced parsley scattered at the top.

[*Mme. Goffaux.*]

POTATOES IN THE BELGIAN MANNER

Take some slices of streaky bacon, about five inches long, and heat them in a pan. When the bacon is half-cooked, take it out of the pan and in the fat that remains behind fry some very finely-sliced onions till they are brown. When the onions are well browned, put them in a large pot, large enough for all the potatoes you wish to cook, adding pepper, salt, and a coffee-spoonful of sweet herbs dried and mixed, which in England replace the thyme and bay-leaves used in Belgium. Add sufficient water to cook the potatoes and your slices of bacon. Cook till tender.

[*E. Wainard.*]

TOMATOES AND SHRIMPS

Lay on a dish some sliced tomatoes, taking out the seeds, and sprinkle them over with picked shrimps. Then pour over all a good mayonnaise sauce. For the sauce: Take the yolk of an egg and mix it with two soup- spoonfuls of salad oil that you must pass in very gently and very little at a time. Melt a good pinch of salt in a teaspoonful of vinegar (tarragon vinegar, if you have it); add pepper and a small quantity of made mustard. In making this sauce be sure to stir it always the same way. It will take about half-an-hour to make it properly.

[*Paquerette.*]

FLEMISH ENDIVE

Choose twelve endives that are short and neat; cut off the outside leaves and pare the bottom; wash them in plenty of water, and cook them in simmering water for three minutes. Then take them from the water and place them in a well-buttered frying-pan, dust them with salt and also with a pinch of sugar. Add the juice of half a lemon, and rather less than a pint of water. Place the pan on the fire for two or three minutes to start the cooking, then cover it closely, and finish the cooking by placing it in the oven for fifty minutes. Take out the endives and put them in the vegetable-dish and pour over them the liquor in which they have been cooked. This liquor is improved by being reduced, and when off the fire, by having a small piece of butter added to it.

The above recipe can be used for chicory as well as for endive.

[*J. Kirckaert.*]

CAULIFLOWER AND SHRIMPS

Take a cauliflower and cut off the green part, and wash it several times in salted water. Boil it gently till cooked, taking care that it remains whole. Put it aside to cool, and when it is quite cold make a hole in the center down to the bottom. Pick some shrimps till you have half a pint of them, make a good mayonnaise and, taking half of it, mix it with the shrimps. Fill the hole in the cauliflower with the shrimps and sauce, and pour the rest of the sauce over the top of the cauliflower.

This dish is to be served very cold.

[*E. Defouck.*]

BELGIAN CARROTS

Clean well the carrots, cut them in dice, and wash them well. Put them on the fire with enough water to cover them, a bit of butter, an onion well minced, salt and pepper and a dessert-spoonful of powdered sugar. Place the dish in the oven for at least an hour, and, when you serve it, sprinkle over the carrots some minced parsley.

[*Gabrielle Janssens.*]

STUFFED TOMATOES

Take ten good tomatoes and cut off the tops, which are to serve as lids. Remove the insides, and fill with the following mixture: minced veal and ham, rather more veal than ham, mushrooms tossed in butter, a little breadcrumb, milk to render it moist, pepper and salt. Put on the covers and add on each one a scrap of butter. Bake them gently in a fireproof dish. The following excellent sauce is poured over them five minutes before taking them out of the oven: Use any stock that you have, preferably veal, adding the insides of the tomatoes, pepper and salt; pass this through the wire sieve. Make a *roux*—that is, melt some butter in a pan, adding flour little by little and stirring until it goes a brown color. Add to it then your tomatoes that have been through the sieve, and some more fried mushrooms. Pour this sauce over the whole and serve very hot.

[*Mme. van Praet.*]

RED CABBAGE

Mince the cabbage and put it in a pan with plenty of refined fat (clarified fat) and two or three large potatoes, pepper and salt. Add sufficient water to cover it, with a dash of vinegar and six dessert-spoonfuls of brown or moist sugar. Let it simmer for four hours, drain it and serve cold.

[*Mme. Segers.*]

VEGETABLE SALAD

The special point of this dish is that peas, beans, carrots in dice, are all cooked separately and when they are cold they are placed in a large dish without being mixed. Decorate with the hearts of lettuce round the edge and with slices of tomato, and pour over it, or hand with it, a good mayonnaise.

[*Mme. van Praet.*]

CHICORY

This excellent vegetable can be dressed either in a bechamel sauce, or with butter and lemon-juice. It is gently stewed, first of all, and it requires pepper and salt. The sauces can be varied with tomato, or with some of the good English bottled sauces stirred with the bechamel.

[*Mme. van Praet.*]

CAULIFLOWER À LA REINE ELIZABETH

Simmer the cauliflowers till tender. Prepare a mince of veal and pork, and season it well with a little spice. Butter a mold and fill it with alternate layers of mince and of cauliflower broken in small pieces. Fill a large saucepan three-quarters full of boiling water and place the mold in this; let it cook for one hour in this way over the fire; turn it out and pour a spinach sauce over it.

[*Mme. van Praet.*]

MUSHROOMS À LA SPINETTE

Make some puff pastry cases, wash and chop the mushrooms and toss them in butter to which you have added a slice of lemon. Make a bechamel sauce with cream, or, failing that, with thick tinned cream, and mix with the mushrooms. Heat the cases for a few minutes in the oven and fill them with the hot mixture.

[*Mme. Spinette.*]

DRESSED CAULIFLOWER

Simmer a cauliflower till it is tender. Pour out the liquor, and add to it a bit of butter, the size of a nut, rolled in flour, a pinch of nutmeg, a tablespoonful of Gruyère cheese and a little milk.

Bind the sauce with a little feculina flour. At the moment of serving, pour the sauce over the cauliflower, which you have placed upright on a dish. The nutmeg and the cheese are indispensable to this dish.

[*V. Verachtert.*]

BRUSSELS SPROUTS

(The best way to cook them)

Having cleaned and trimmed your sprouts, let them simmer in salted water, to which you have also added a little soda to preserve the color. Or, if you do not like to add soda, keep the pan firmly covered by the lid. When tender, take them out and let them drain, place them in another pan with a good lump of butter or fat; stir, so as to let the butter melt at once, and sprinkle in pepper and a tiny pinch of nutmeg.

[*Mdlle. Germaine Verstraete.*]

RAGOUT OF MUTTON

Fry the mutton very well. Then place in another pan sufficient water to cover your mutton, adding pepper, salt, a little nutmeg, a celery, and a few white turnips cut in pieces. When they are well cooked, add the meat and let all simmer for two hours.

[*V. Verachtert.*]

STEWED SHOULDER OF MUTTON

Put in a pan a large lump of butter or clarified fat, and place the shoulder in it. Add two big onions sliced, and a very large carrot also sliced, thyme, bay-leaf, two cloves, pepper and salt, and, if you like it, two garlic knobs. Let the shoulder simmer in this by the side of the fire for three hours. Strain the sauce through a fine sieve, and then add to it either a glass of good red wine or a little made mustard with a teaspoonful of brown sugar.

[*Mme. Segers.*]

SHOULDER OF MUTTON

Put a handful of dried white haricots to soak over-night and simmer them the following day for two hours with some salt. Rub your shoulder of mutton with a little bit of garlic before putting it in the oven to cook, and when it is done, serve with the haricots round it, to which have been added a pat or two of butter.

[*V. Verachtert.*]

MUTTON COLLOPS

Take some slices of roast or boiled leg of mutton, egg them, and roll in a mixture of breadcrumbs, salt, pepper, and a little flower. Fry till the slices are brown on each side; serve with chipped potatoes.

SHOULDER OF MUTTON DRESSED LIKE KID

My readers have probably tasted a shoulder of kid dressed as mutton. Let them therefore try the converse of the dish, and, if they really take trouble with it, they will have a dinner of the most delicious. Put into a deep dish that will hold your shoulder of mutton the following mixture:

A cupful each of oil, vinegar, white wine, red wine, an onion stuffed with cloves, a bunch of herbs which must be fresh ones—thyme, parsley, marjoram, sage, a tiny bit of mint, a few bay-leaves—two medium carrots cut in slices. Put the shoulder of mutton in this mixture and keep it there for four days, turning it every now and then and pouring the mixture on it. On the fifth day take it out, and, if you care to take the trouble, you will improve it by larding the meat here and there. Put it to roast in front of a good fire, with your liquor, which serves to baste it with, in a pan beneath. If you cannot arrange to hang the mutton by a string to turn like a roasting jack, then bake it, and continually baste it. A small shoulder is most successful. For one of four pounds bake for fifty minutes.

ROAST RUMP OF BEEF, BORDELAISE SAUCE

Take three pounds of the rump of beef, put it into a pretty deep pan upon one onion, one sliced carrot, some thyme, and a bay-leaf, three table- spoonfuls of dripping, salt, and pepper. Put it on the top of the fire, and when it comes fully to the boil, put it to the side, and allow it to simmer nicely for an hour and a half. Dress it on a dish and serve the sauce separately.

ROASTED FILLET OF BEEF

About three pounds of fillet of beef roasted in a good hot oven for forty minutes; let it be rather underdone. Take three turnips, four good-sized carrots, cut them into jardinière slices. Cook them separately in salted water, drain them and add salt, pepper, a tiny pinch of sugar and one dessert-spoonful of butter. Dress the fillet on a long dish with the garniture of carrots and turnips, and some artichoke-bottoms cooked in water and finished with butter, also add some potatoes *château*. Be sure the dish is very hot. Put a little water, or, for choice, clear stock, upon the roasting-dish and pour it over the fillet.

BEEF À LA BOURGUIGNONNE

Braise three pounds of beef upon twenty little onions, ten mushrooms, and two glasses of red wine, salt, pepper, thyme and bay-leaf; cook for one and one-half hours with not too hot a fire. After that, place the beef on an oval dish; keep it hot; stir two tablespoonfuls of demi-glaze into the vegetables and let it boil up. Cut some slices of the beef, and strain the sauce over all.

OX-TONGUE À LA BOURGEOISE

Braise a tongue with two glasses of Madeira, one carrot, one onion, thyme, bay-leaf, for two hours. Take seven tomatoes cut in pieces, four carrots cut in two and three in four, about one-half inch long, ten smallish onions, and braise them all together; then add two large table- spoonfuls of demi-glaze, some salt and pepper. Serve all very hot on an oval dish.

Braised tongue eats very well with spinach, carrots or sorrel.

BEEF À LA MODE

Take the raw beef, either rump-steak or fillet, and brown it in the pan in some butter. Then add a little boiling water. Add then six or eight chopped shallots, the hearts of two celeries chopped, a few small and whole carrots, pepper, salt, two cloves. Before serving, bind the sauce with a little flour and pour all over the meat.

[V. Verachtert.]

BOEUF À LA FLAMANDE

For this national dish that part of the animal called the "spiering" is used, which is cut from near the neck. What is called fresh silverside in England answers very well. Cut the beef into slices about half-an-inch thick and divide the slices into four pieces. This you can do with a piece of four pounds. For a piece of four pounds, cook first of all four large fried onions in fat. Put the beef in the hot fat when the onions are colored, and sauté it; that is, keep moving the meat about gently. Take the meat out and place it on a dish. Add to the fat two dessert- spoonsful of flour and let it cook gently for five minutes, adding a good pint of water. Pass the sauce through a tammy, over the onions, and put the meat back in it, and it ought to cover them. Then add a dessert- spoonful of good vinegar and a strong bunch of herbs. Stew for an hour, take off the fat and remove the bunch of herbs. Heat up again and serve.

CARETAKER'S BEEF

The real name of this dish is *Miroton de la Concierge*, and it is currently held that only *concierges* can do it to perfection. Put a handful of minced onion to fry in butter; when it is nearly cooked, but not quite, add a dessert-spoonful of flour, and stir it till all is well colored. Pour on it a little gravy, or meat-juice of some kind, and let it simmer for ten minutes after it begins to steam again. Then take your beef, which must be cold, and cut in small slices; throw them in and let it all cook for a quarter of an hour, only simmering, and constantly stirring it, so that though it becomes considerably reduced it does not stick to the pan.

BLANKENBERG BEEF

This is a winter dish; it is most sustaining, and once made, it can be kept hot for hours without spoiling. Make a purée of lentils or peas, and season it with pepper and salt. Mince your beef with an equal quantity of peeled chestnuts, add chopped parsley, a dust of nutmeg or a few cloves. If you have any cheap red wine pour it over the mince till it is well moistened. If you have no red wine, use gravy. If you have no gravy, use milk. Let all heat up in the oven for ten minutes, then sprinkle in some currants or sultanas. Take the dish you wish to serve it in, put the stew in the middle, and place the purée round it. If the mince is moist it can be kept by the fire till required, or the dish can be covered with another one and placed in a carrying-can, taken out to skating or shooting parties.

VEAL WITH TOMATOES

Grill some slices of fat veal; cook some sliced tomatoes with butter, pepper and salt, on a flat dish in a pretty quick oven. Garnish the veal with the tomatoes laid on top of each slice, and pour *maître-d'h'tel* butter over, made with butter, salt, chopped parsley, and lemon-juice.

FRICANDEAU OF VEAL

A fillet of veal, larded with fat bacon, of about three pounds. Braise it one and one-half hours on a moderate fire. Dish with its own gravy. This eats well with spinach, endive, sorrel or carrots.

VEAL CUTLETS WITH MADEIRA SAUCE

are garnished with potatoes and mushrooms, and the sauce is made of demi- glaze and madeira, worked up with butter, pepper, salt and chopped parsley.

GRENADINS OF VEAL

Cut your veal into fairly thick cutlets, lard them with fat bacon, and braise them in the oven, with salt, pepper and butter. Dish up, and rinse the pot with a little stock, and pour it on the meat ready to serve.

CALF'S LIVER À LA BOURGEOISE

Take a calf's liver, lard it with fat bacon, braise it with the *bourgeoise* garnish—carrots and turnips. After it is cooked and dished, stir some demi-glaze into the sauce, pour it on to the meat and garnish with potatoes *château*.

VEAL WITH MUSHROOMS, OR THE CALF IN PARADISE

Take some slices of loin of veal, fry them in butter, with pepper and salt, for twenty minutes. Take two spoonfuls of demi-glaze and heat it with some mushrooms and a little madeira. Put the mushrooms and sauce on each slice and sprinkle chopped parsley over all.

This can also be done with *fines herbes*, mushrooms, chervil and parsley, chopped before cooking them in the butter.

BLANQUETTE OF VEAL

Take your veal, which need not be from the fillet or the best cuts. Cut it into pieces about an inch long and add a little water when putting it into the pan; salt, pepper and a little nutmeg, and let it simmer for two hours. When tender, stir in the juice of half a lemon, and then bind the sauce with the yolk of an egg, or, in default of that, with a little flour. Serve immediately. You will find that when you wish to bind a sauce at the last minute, egg powder will serve very well.

[*V. Verachtert.*]

VEAL CAKE, EXCELLENT FOR SUPPER

Take some chopped veal and with it an equal quantity of chopped beef, and one-quarter the quantity of breadcrumbs from a fresh loaf. Bind all with a raw egg, adding salt and pepper, and, if wished, some blanched and chopped almonds. (Put a large piece of butter both above and below.) Shape the meat into the form of a loaf and put it in a dish, with a large slice of butter above and below it. Cook it for about half-an-hour.

[*Mme. Gabrielle Janssens.*]

BREAST OF VEAL

(A good and inexpensive dish)

Cook the breast of veal in stock or in a little meat extract and water, with sliced carrots and onions, thyme, pepper, salt, three bay-leaves and three cloves. Let it stew for one hour in this, and then take it out. Take out also the vegetables, and strain the liquor. Make a bechamel sauce and add it to the liquor, giving it all a sharp taste with the juice of half a lemon. Put back the breast of veal in this sauce and when hot again serve them together.

[*Mdlle. Spinette.*]

OX TONGUE

Cook the ox tongue in stock or in meat extract and water. Make the hunters' sauce, as for a hare, but sprinkle into it some chopped sultanas. Take the tongue out of the stock and skin it, cut it in neat pieces if you wish, and let it heat in your sauce.

[*Mdlle. Spinette.*]

VEAL À LA MILANAISE

Egg and breadcrumb some thick slices of veal; fry and garnish with boiled macaroni cut in small pieces, with ham, mushrooms, truffles, all cut in Julienne strips, pepper, salt, and a little tomato sauce. Mix all these well together, and serve very hot.

STUFFED VEAL LIVER, OR LIVER À LA PANIER D'OR

The *Panier d'Or* is a hotel in Bruges, much frequented before the war by the English.

Take the yolk of a hard-boiled egg, a bit of bread the same size, and crumble them together; rub in some chopped parsley and onion and moisten it with gravy or with milk; season highly with salt, cayenne, and a little vinegar or mustard. Take your liver, if possible in one rather large flat slice. Make deep cuts in it, parallel to each other, and lying closely together. Press your stuffing into these cuts. Put a bit of butter the size of a walnut into a pan, or fireproof dish. Take your liver and tie it round with a slice of fat bacon or fat pork. Lay it in the dish and let it cook for an hour in a moderate oven. When done, remove the slice of bacon, if there is any left, and serve the liver in its own juice.

VEAL À LA CRÊME

Take a piece of veal suitable for roasting, and put it in vinegar for twenty-four hours.

Roast it with butter, pepper and salt, with a few slices of onion. Baste it well, and when it is finished crush the onions in the gravy and add some cream. Mix together with flour so as to thicken.

[*Mdlle. Spreakers.*]

This is the demi-glaze Sauce which is used for all brown Sauces.

Take one pound of flour, dry it in the oven on a tray till it is the color of cocoa; pass it through a sieve into a saucepan, moisten it with stock, mixing very carefully. Boil it up two or three times during forty- eight hours, adding two carrots, two onions, thyme, bay, all cut up, which you have colored in the frying-pan, also some salt and peppercorns. When it is all cooked, pass it through a cloth or sieve. When it is reduced the first time, you should add some stock, but by the time it is finished it should be fairly thick. It will keep for a fortnight.

[*G. Goffaux.*]

DUTCH SAUCE FOR FISH

Take a tablespoonful of flour and three of water; make it boil and add the yolks of three eggs; melt one-half pound of butter and beat it gently into your first mixture, add salt, the juice of half a lemon and a pinch of grated nutmeg. Keep the sauce very hot in a *bain-marie* or in a double saucepan. If you have neither, keep it in a large cup placed in a saucepan of hot water.

[*Mrs. Emelie Jones.*]

BEARNAISE SAUCE

(Very good with stewed meat)

Put some onions to cook in tarragon vinegar and water; when they are half done, add more water and throw in a little thyme and a leaf or two of bay; let it cook for one hour and pass it through a sieve. Melt some butter in a pan and thicken it with flour; put your vinegar to it and more water if you think it necessary; stir in salt and pepper and the yolks of two eggs or more, according to the quantity that you wish to make. Let it get thick, and just as you take it off the fire add a sprinkle of chopped parsley and a pat of butter. This is a useful sauce and it well repays the trouble.

[*Mme. Spinette.*]

MUSLIN SAUCE

Melt a piece of butter the size of an egg, sprinkle and stir in some flour, adding water if it becomes too thick. Keep stirring over the fire for five minutes, and, still stirring, add pepper and salt and the yolks of two eggs. You may add the yolks of three or four eggs if you wish for a rich sauce. The last item is the juice of a lemon to your taste. This is a very popular addition to meat.

[*Mme. Spinette.*]

SAUCE BORDELAISE

Two shallots, ten tarragon leaves all chopped, are put into a very small saucepan. Add a large glass of claret, a dessert-spoonful of butter, and let it all reduce together. Add salt, pepper, three dessert-spoonfuls of demi-glaze, let it come to the boil, and stir in two dessert-spoonfuls of butter.

[*Georges Goffaux.*]

POOR MAN'S SAUCE

Even a piece of meat of poor quality is much liked if it has the following sauce poured over it when served. Put a little milk, say a cupful, in a saucepan, with salt and pepper; let it heat. Chop up a handful of shallots and a quarter as much of parsley that is well washed. Throw them into the milk; let it boil, and when the shallots are tender the sauce is ready. If you have no milk, use water; but in that case let it be strongly flavored with vinegar.

THE GOOD WIFE'S SAUCE

This sauce is indispensable to any one who wishes to use up slices of cold mutton. Trim your slices, take away skin and fat and pour on them the following cold sauce. Hard-boil three eggs, let them get cold. Crumble the yolks in a cup, adding slowly a tablespoonful of oil, salt, pepper, a little mustard, a teaspoonful of vinegar; then chop the whites of egg, with a scrap of onion, and if you have them, some capers. Mix all together and pour it over the cold meat.

CREAM SAUCE

Roll a lump of butter in flour, put it in a pan on the fire, and as it melts add pepper and salt. Stir it, and as it thickens add a little milk; let it simmer and keep on stirring it. You will never get a good white sauce unless you season it well and let it simmer for a quarter of an hour. Strain it, heat it again, and serve it for fish, potatoes, chicken.

SAUCE MAÎTRE D'HÔTEL

Every one likes this sauce for either meat or fish. In a double saucepan melt a lump of butter, flavor it with salt, pepper, some minced parsley that you had first rubbed on a raw slice of onion, and some lemon-juice. Use vinegar instead of the lemon if you wish, but do not forget that it does not require so much vinegar. Mix it with a fork and serve it warm; do not let it bubble.

SAUCE AU DIABLE

(For cold meats)

Take a shallot or two, according to quantity of sauce needed, slice very finely, shred a little parsley, put both into the sauce-boat, with salt, pepper, and mustard to taste; add oil and vinegar in proportion of one dessert-spoonful of vinegar to two table-spoonfuls of oil, till sufficient quantity.

FRICASSEE OF PIGEONS

Put your pieces of pigeon into a stew-pan in butter, and let it cook with the pigeons. Then add one carrot, two onions, two sprigs of parsley, a leaf of sage, five juniper berries, and a very little nutmeg. Stir it all for a few minutes, and then, and only then, add a half-cupful of water and Liebig, two rusks or dry biscuits in pieces, the juice of a lemon. Put it all on the side of the fire, cover the saucepan and let it cook gently for an hour and a half.

[*Mme. Vandervalle.*]

HUNTER'S HARE

Cut the hare in pieces and cook it in the oven in butter, pepper and salt, turning it now and then so that it does not get dry. Then prepare

Hunter's Sauce. Melt a bit of butter the size of an egg and add flour, letting it brown, fry in it plenty of chopped onions and shallots, adding tarragon vinegar, cayenne and pepper-corns; spice it highly with nutmeg, three cloves, a sprig of thyme and a couple of bay-leaves. Chop up the hare liver, put it in the sauce and pass all through the sieve. Pour the sauce over the hare and add a good glass of claret, or, for English tastes, of port wine. If the sauce is too thin, thicken it with flour, and serve all together.

[*Mme. Spinette.*]

FLEMISH RABBIT

Cut the rabbit into neat pieces. Put them into a deep frying-pan and toss them in butter, so that each piece is well browned without burning the butter. Take them out of the pan and in the same butter cook six shallots (finely minced) till they are brown. Then return the rabbit to the pan, seasoning all with salt and pepper, adding as well three bay-leaves, two cloves, and two white peppers. If you have any gravy, add a pint of it, but in default of gravy add the same quantity of Bovril and water. Place on the fire till it boils, then draw it to the side and let it cook there gently for three-quarters of an hour. Just when it is nearly done, add a little vinegar, more or less according to your taste. This is served with boiled and well-drained potatoes. If the sauce is not thick enough, add to it a little flour which has been first mixed with some cold water.

[*Georges Kerckeert.*]

ROAST KID WITH VENISON SAUCE

This dish is very excellent with mutton instead of kid; the meat tastes like venison if this recipe is followed:

Put the meat, say a shoulder of mutton, to soak in a bottle of red wine, with a sliced carrot, thyme, bay-leaves (4), six cloves, fifteen peppercorns and a teaspoonful of vinegar, for two hours. Then bring the liquor to the boil and just before it is boiling pour it over and over the meat. Do this pouring over of hot liquor for two days. Then put the meat in the oven with butter, pepper, and salt, till it is cooked.

Sauce: Brown some onions in butter and pour in your liquor, but without the carrot. Let it simmer for three-quarters of an hour, and pour it through a sieve. Roll a nut of butter in flour and add little by little the liquor you have from the meat, then a coffee-spoonful of meat extract and two lumps of sugar. This sauce ought to be quite thick. It is served with the meat. [*Mme. Vandervalle.*]

BAKED RABBIT

Fry the pieces of rabbit, adding three onions, two medium potatoes, half a glass of beer, a little water or stock, pepper and salt. Let it all bake gently in an earthenware pot for two hours, and then thicken the same with flour. It is an improvement to add when it is being cooked two cloves, two bay-leaves, a pinch of nutmeg, and any fresh herbs, such as thyme, parsley, mint.

[*Mme. E. Maes.*]

CHICKEN À LA MAX

Chop up some cold chicken into small squares, mix with a thick white sauce, and let it heat. Put it on a hot dish and cover with fried onions. Put chipped potatoes at the ends of the dish and a boiled chicory at either side. This excellent dish has received distinction also from its name, that of the heroic and ingenious burgomaster of Brussels.

[*M. Stuart.*]

RABBIT À LA BORDELAISE

Cut a rabbit into joints, cover with vinegar, chop finely two small onions, thyme, pepper, and salt, and a little grated nutmeg; let all soak for twenty-four hours.

Take out the joints and brown gently in a little dripping; when all are nicely browned take one cupful of the marmalade and stew till tender one and a half to two hours. When ready, strain off the sauce, thicken nicely with flour, dish the rabbit, and pour over the sauce.

LAEKEN RABBIT

Take a medium-sized rabbit, and have it prepared and cut into joints. Put the pieces to soak for forty-eight hours in vinegar, enough to cover them, with a sprinkle of fresh thyme in it and a small onion sliced finely. After forty-eight hours, put one-quarter pound of fat bacon, sliced, in a pan to melt, and when it has melted, take out any bits that remain, and add to the melted bacon a bit of butter as big as an egg, which let melt till it froths; secondly, sprinkle in a dessert-spoonful of flour. Stir it over the fire, mixing well till the sauce becomes brown, and then put in your marinaded pieces of rabbit. Add pepper and salt and cook till each piece is well colored on each side. When they are well colored, add then the bunch of thyme, the sliced onion and half the vinegar that you used for soaking; three bay-leaves, one dozen dried and dry prunes, five lumps of sugar, half a pint of water. Cover closely and let it simmer for two hours and a half.

[*A Belgian at Droitwich.*]

RABBIT

Put the back and the hind legs of one or two rabbits in an oven, covering the same first with a layer of butter (half inch thick) and then with a layer of French mustard, pepper and salt. Roast by a good fire for one hour, baste often with the juice from the meat and the gravy.

HARE

To be put in a pan in the oven: sauce, butter, and a quarter of a pint of cream, pepper, salt and some flour to thicken the sauce. Before the hare is put in the oven, cover it with a thin piece of bacon, which must be taken away before the hare is brought to table.

[*Mdlle. Breakers.*]

RUM OMELETTE

This simple dish is much liked by gentlemen. Break five eggs in a basin, sweeten them with castor sugar, pour in a sherry glassful of rum. Beat them very hard till they froth. Put a bit of fresh butter in a shallow pan and pour in your eggs. Let it stay on the fire just three minutes and then slip it off on to a hot dish. Powder it with sugar, as you take it to the dining-room. At the dining-room door, set a light to a big spoonful of rum and pour it over the omelette just as you go in. It is almost impossible to light a glass of rum in a hurry, for your omelette, so use a kitchen spoon.

THE CHILDREN'S BIRTHDAY DISH

Boil up a quart of milk, sweeten it with nearly half a pound of sugar, and flavor with vanilla. Let it get cold. Beat up six eggs, both yolks and whites, mix them with the milk, put it all in a fireproof dish and cook very gently. Cover the top before you serve it with ratafia biscuits.

A FRANGIPANI

Put your saucepan on the table and break in it two eggs. Mix these with two dessertspoonfuls of flour. Add a pint of milk, and put it on the fire, stirring always one way. Let it cook for a quarter of an hour, stirring with one hand, while with the other sprinkle in powdered sugar and ground almonds. Turn out to get cold, and cut in squares.

APRICOT SOUFFLÉ

This is good enough even for an English "dinner-party. " Beat the whites of six eggs stiffly. Take four dessert-spoonfuls of apricot jam, or an equal quantity of those dried apricots that have been soaked and stewed to a purée. If you use jam, you need not add sugar. If you use the dried apricots, add sugar to sweeten. Butter a dish at the bottom, and when you have well mixed with a fork the beaten whites and the apricot, put it in a pyramid on the dish and bake for fifteen minutes in a moderate oven. Powder with sugar.

STEWED PRUNES

Prunes are very good done this way. Take a pound of prunes, soak them twenty-four hours in water. Put them on the fire in a cupful of water and half a bottle of light red wine, quarter of a pound of sugar and, if you like it, a pinch of cinnamon or mixed spice. Let it all stew till the liquor is much reduced and the prunes are well flavored. Let them get cold, and serve them in a glass dish with whipped cream.

CHOCOLATE CREAM

Take the whites of six eggs and beat them stiff, doing first one and then another, adding to them three soup-spoonfuls of powdered sugar and three sticks of chocolate that you have grated. If you have powdered chocolate by you, use that, and taste the mixture to judge when it is well flavored. Mix it all well in a cool place. To do this dish successfully, make it just before you wish to serve it.

[*Mdlle. Lust, of Brussels.*]

SEMOLINA SOUFFLÉ

Boil up two pints of milk and fifteen lumps of sugar with a bit of vanilla. Add three soup-spoonfuls of semolina, and let it boil for fifteen minutes, while you stir it. Take it from the fire, and add to it the yolks of two eggs and their whites that you have beaten stiffly. Put it in the oven for a quarter of an hour, and serve it hot.

[*Mdlle. Lust, of Brussels.*]

SNOWY MOUNTAINS

Butter six circular rusks, and put on them a layer of jam. Beat the whites of three eggs and place them on the rusks in the shape of a pyramide. Put them in the oven and color a little. They must be served hot.

[*Mdlle. Lust, of Brussels.*]

RICHELIEU RICE

Put three soup-spoonfuls of Carolina rice to swell in a little water, with a pat of butter. When the rice has absorbed all the water, add a pint of milk, sugar to sweeten, a few raisins, some chopped orange-peel, and some crystallized cherries, or any other preserved fruit. Put all on the fire, and when the mixture is cooked the rice ought to be creamy. Add the yolk of an egg, stir it well, and pour all into a mold. Put it to cool. Turn it out, and serve it with the following sauce, which must be poured on the shape.

A pint of milk, sugar, and vanilla; let it boil. Stir a soup-spoonful of cornflour in water till it is smooth, mix it with the boiling milk, let it boil while stirring it for a few minutes, take it from the fire, add the yolk of an egg, and pour it on the rice shape. Serve when cold.

[*Mdlle. Lust, of Brussels.*]

EXCELLENT PASTE FOR PASTRY

Equal quantities of butter and flour, well mixed in a little beer; add also a pinch of salt. Make this paste the day before you require it; it is good for little patties and tarts.

[*Mdlle. Le Kent.*]

CHOCOLATE CREAM

(No. 2)

Melt four penny tablets of chocolate in hot milk until it is liquid and without lumps. Boil up a pint of milk with a stick of vanilla, a big lump of butter (size of a walnut) and ten lumps of sugar. When this boils, add the chocolate and keep stirring continually. Then take the yolks of three eggs and well beat them; it is better to have these beaten before, so as not to interfere with the stirring of your mixture. Add your three yolks and keep on stirring, always in the same way. Then pour the mixture into a mold that has been rinsed out in very cold water, and let it stand in a cool place till set.

[*Mrs. Emelie Jones.*]

BELGIAN GINGERBREAD

1/2 pound cornflour
1/4 pound butter
1/4 pound white sugar
1 or 2 eggs
1/2 ounce ginger powder.

Work all the ingredients together on a marble slab, to get the paste all of the same consistency. Make it into balls as big as walnuts, flattening them slightly before putting them into the oven. This sort of gingerbread keeps very well.

[*L. L. B. d'Anvers.*]

APPLE FRITTERS

Put half pound of flour in a deep dish and work it with beer, beating it well till there are no lumps left. Make it into a paste that is not very liquid. Peel and core some good apples, cut them into rounds, put them in the paste so that each one is well covered with it. Have a pan of boiling fat and throw in the apple slices for two minutes. They ought to be golden by then, if that fat has been hot enough. Serve them dusted with powdered sugar and the juice of half a lemon squeezed on them.

[*Mme. Delahaye.*]

FOUR QUARTERS

Weigh four very fresh eggs and put them in an earthenware dish. Add successively, sieved flour, fine sugar, and fresh butter, each one of these items being of the same weight of the eggs—hence the name: Four Quarters. With a wooden spoon, work these four ingredients, then let them rest for five minutes. Turn it all into a buttered mold and let it cook for five quarters of an hour in a gentle oven or in a double saucepan. Turn it out, and eat it either cold or hot and with fruit.

[*Georges Kerckaert.*]

SAFFRON RICE

Wash the rice in cold water, heat it in a little water and add a dust of salt. Flavor some milk (enough to cover the rice) with vanilla, and pour it on the rice. Let it cook in the oven for an hour and a quarter. Take it from the fire, and stir in the yolks only of two eggs, or of one only, if wished. Sweeten the whole with sugar, and color it with a little saffron. Turn it out, and let it get very cold.

[*Paquerette.*]

SEMOLINA FRITTERS

Quarter pound semolina, one and a half pints of milk, three eggs. Put on the milk, and, as soon as it is boiling, drop the semolina in, in a shower. Let it boil for a few minutes, stirring continually. Then add the yolks of three eggs, and then the whites, which you have already beaten stiff. Pour all on a dish, and cool. Have some boiling lard (it is boiling when it ceases to bubble), and throw into it spoonsful of the mixture. When they are fried golden, take them out, drain them a moment, and sprinkle on some white sugar.

[*Mme. Segers.*]

SPECULOOS

(A Brussels recipe)

Pound down half pound flour, four ounces brown sugar, three and a half ounces butter, a pinch of nutmeg, and the same of mace and cinnamon in powder. Add, as well, a pinch of bicarbonate of soda. Make the paste into a ball, and cover it with a fine linen or muslin cloth, and leave it till the following day. If you have no molds to press it in, cut it into diamonds or different shapes, and cook them in the oven on buttered trays. I believe waffle irons can be bought in London.

GAUFRES FROM BRUSSELS

Mix in an earthern bowl half a pint of flour, five yolks of eggs, a coffee-spoonful of castor sugar, half pint of milk (fresh), adding a pinch of salt and of vanilla; then two ounces butter melted over hot water. Then beat up the whites of four eggs very stiffly, and add them. Butter a baking-tin or sheet (since English households have not got a gaufre-iron, which is double and closes up), and pour in your mixture, spreading it over the sheet. When the gaufre is nicely yellowed, take it out and powder it with sugar. But to render this recipe absolutely successful, the correct implement is necessary.

RICE À LA CONDE

Simmer the rice in milk till it is tender, sweeten it, and add, for a medium-sized mold, the yolks of two eggs. Let it thicken a little, and stir in pieces of pineapple. Pour it into a mold, and let it cool. Turn it out when it has well set, and decorate with crystallized fruits. Pour round it a thin apricot syrup.

[*Mme. Spinette.*]

PAINS PERDUS

(Lost bread)

Make a mixture of milk and raw eggs, enough to soak up in six rusks. Flavor it with a little mace or cinnamon. Put some butter in a pan and put the rusks in it to fry. Let them color a good brown, and serve them hot with sugar dusted over them.

[*Mme. Spinette.*]

FRUIT FRITTERS

Peel some apples, take out the core and cut them in slices, powder them on each side with sugar. You can use also pears, melons, or bananas. Make a batter with flour, milk and eggs, beating well the whites; a glass of rum and sugar to sweeten it. Put your lard on to heat, and when the blue steam rises roll your fruit slices in the batter and throw them into the lard. When they are golden, serve them with powdered sugar.

[*Mme. Spinette.*]

MOCHA CAKE

Take half a pound of fresh butter, four ounces of powdered sugar, and work them well together. When they are well mixed, add the yolks of four eggs, each one separately, and the whites of two. When the mixture is thoroughly well done, add, drop by drop, some boiling coffee essence to your taste. Butter a mold and line it with small sponge biscuits, and fill it with alternate layers of the cream and of biscuits. Put it for the night in the cellar before you serve it the following day. You can replace the essence of coffee by some chocolate that has been melted over hot water.

[*Mme. Spinette.*]

VANILLA CREAM

Sweeten well half a pint of milk and flavor it with vanilla. Put it to boil. Mix in a dish the yolks of four eggs with a little cornflour. When the milk boils, pour it very slowly over the eggs, mixing it well. Return it all to the pan and let it get thick without bringing it to the boil. Add some chopped almonds, and turn the mixture into a mold to cool.

[*Mme. Spinette.*]

RUM CREAM

Take sponge biscuits and arrange them on a dish, joining each to the other with jam. (You can make a square or a circle or a sort of hollow tower.) Pour your rum over them till they are well soaked. Then pour over them, or into the middle of the biscuits, a vanilla cream like the foregoing recipe, but let it be nearly cold before you use it. Decorate the top with the whites of four eggs sweetened and beaten, or use fresh cream in the same way.

[*Mme. Spinette.*]

PINEAPPLE À L'ANVERS

Take some slices of pineapple, and cut off the brown spots at the edges. Steep them for three hours in a plateful of weak kirsch, or maraschino, that is slightly warmed. Cut some slices of plain cake of equal thickness, and glaze them. This is done by sprinkling sugar over the slices and placing them in a gentle oven. The sugar melts and leaves the slices *glacés*. Arrange the slices in a circle, alternating pineapple and cake, and pour over the latter an apricot marmalade thinned with kirsch or other liqueur. This dish looks very nice, and if whipped cream can be added it is excellent.

[*L. L. B. Anvers.*]

POUDING AUX POMMES

Take a pound of apples and peel them. Cook them, and rub them, when soft, through a sieve to make them into a purée. Sweeten it well, and scent it with a scrap of vanilla; then let it get cold. Beat up three eggs, both whites and yolks, and mix them into your cold comp'te, and put all in a dish that will stand the heat of the oven. Then place on the top a bit of butter the size of a filbert and powder all over with white sugar. Place the dish in an oven with a gentle heat for half-an-hour, watching how it cooks. This dish can be eaten hot or cold.

[*E. Defouck.*]

SOUFFLÉ AU CHOCOLAT

Melt two tablets of chocolate (Menier) in a dessert-spoonful of water over heat, stirring till the chocolate is well wetted and very thick. Then prepare some feculina flour in the following way: Take for five or six persons nearly a pint of milk. Sweeten it well with sugar; take two dessert-spoonfuls of feculina. Boil the sweetened milk, flavoring it with a few drops of vanilla essence. When it is boiled, take it from the fire, and let it get cold, mixing in the flour by adding it slowly so as not to make lumps. Put it back on a brisk fire and stir till it thickens; add then the melted chocolate, and when that is gently stirred in take off your pan, and again let it get cold. At the moment of cooking the soufflé, add three whites of eggs beaten stiff. Butter a deep fireproof dish, and pour in the mixture, only filling up half of the dish. Cook in the oven for fifteen minutes in a gentle heat, and serve immediately. A tablet of Chocolat Menier is a recognized weight.

[*Gabrielle Janssens.*]

A NEW DISH OF APPLES

Take a pint of apple purée and add to it three well-beaten eggs, a taste of cinnamon if liked, quarter of a pound of melted butter and the same quantity of white powdered sugar. Mix all together and, taking a fireproof dish, put a little water in the bottom of it and then some fine breadcrumbs, sufficient to cover the bottom. Pour in your comp'te, then, above that, a layer of fine breadcrumbs, and here and there a lump of fresh butter, which will prevent the breadcrumbs from burning. Cook for half-an-hour.

GOLDEN RICE

Put a quart of milk to boil, and, when boiling, add half a pound of good rice. When the rice is nearly cooked, add a pennyworth of saffron, stirring it in evenly. This is excellent, eaten cold with stewed quinces and cream.

[*V. Verachtert.*]

BANANA COMPÔTE

Divide the bananas in regular pieces; arrange them in slices on your comp'te dish, one slice leaning against the other in a circle. Sprinkle them with sugar. Squeeze the juice of an orange and of half a lemon—this would be sufficient for six bananas—and pour it over the bananas. Cover the dish and leave it for two hours in a cold place. A mold of cornflour or of ground rice may be eaten with this.

[*Mme. Gabrielle Janssens.*]

RIZ CONDE

For one and one-half pints of milk half a breakfast-cupful of rice. Let it boil with sugar and vanilla; strain the whole. Add one-half pint of cream, well beaten, five leaves of gelatine (melted). Mix the whole and pour in a mold which has been wet. When turned out of the mold, put apricots or other fruit on the top. Pour the juice over all.

[*Mlle. Breakers.*]

CHOCOLATE CREAM

10 leaves of gelatine, well melted and sifted. 1 pint cream, *well beaten*. 3-1/2 sticks of chocolate melted with a little milk.

Mix all the ingredients together and put them in a mold which has been previously wet.

[*Mlle. Breakers.*]

KIDNEY SOUFFLÉ

Mince finely a veal kidney and add one-half pound of minced veal. Make a brown sauce of flour and butter, and add the meat to it. Let it cool a little, and add three well-beaten eggs, with a teaspoonful of rasped Gruyère. Butter a mold, and sprinkle the inside with breadcrumbs, and fill it with the mince. Leave it for three quarters of an hour in the oven, or for an hour and a half in the double saucepan of boiling water. Turn it out of the mold and serve with either a tomato or a mushroom sauce.

[*L. L. B. (d'Anvers).*]

BAKED SOUFFLE

Three eggs, two table-spoonfuls of powdered sugar and a thimbleful of cornflour or feculina flour. The original recipe gives also one packet of vanilla sugar, but as this may be difficult to get in England it will be easier to add a few drops of vanilla essence when mixing. Mix the yolks of eggs with the sugar for ten minutes, then add the whites, stiffly beaten, stirring in very lightly, so as to let as much air as possible remain in the mixture; sprinkle in the flour. Take a fireproof dish, and butter it, and pour in the mixture, which place in a gentle oven for a quarter of an hour. It is better to practice this recipe at lest once before you prepare it at a dinner, on account of the baking.

[*L. Verhaeghe.*]

PEASANTS' EGGS

For six people put on the fire two handfuls of sorrel, reduce it to a puree, and add two dessertspoonfuls of cream, a lump of butter the size of a pigeon's egg, pepper, salt. Take six hard-boiled eggs and, crumbling out the yolks, add them to the sorrel puree. Place the whites (which you should have cut longways) on a hot dish, and pour over them the puree of sorrel; sprinkle the top with breadcrumbs, and put bits of butter on it also. Place in the oven for ten minutes, and serve garnished with tomatoes.

[*Mlle. A. Demeulemeester.*]

TWO RECIPES FOR TOMATOES AND EGGS

Take some good tomatoes, but not too ripe. Cut them down from top to bottom, take out the pulp, and in each half tomato put half a hard-boiled egg. Arrange them on a dish, and pour round them a good mayonnaise, to which you have added some chopped parsley.

Take some tomatoes not too ripe, and cut them in half horizontally. Take out the pulp, so that you have two half-cases from each tomato. Break an egg into each tomato and sprinkle it well with cheese. Place them all in the oven, till the eggs are set, and decorate with sprigs of parsley.

[Mlle. A. Demeulemeester.]

TOMATOES AND EGGS

Hard-boil some eggs and, while they are cooking, fry a large square slice of bread in butter to make a large crouton. Peel the eggs when they have been in boiling water for ten minutes. Pile them on the crouton, and have ready a tomato sauce to pour over.

Tomato Sauce: Gently stew two pounds of tomatoes and pass them through a sieve, return them to the pan and stir in a mustard-spoonful of mustard, a teaspoonful of vinegar, salt and pepper; heat well; and, if too thin, thicken it with flour to the right consistency.

[*Mme. van Praet.*]

MUSHROOM OMELETTE

Toss the sliced mushrooms in butter, adding, if you wish, a little mushroom ketchup. Break the eggs in a pan and beat them lightly together, and cook for three minutes over a good fire. Slip the omelette on a hot dish, spread with butter.

ASPARAGUS OMELETTE

This is made quite differently. Cook the asparagus-tops in salt and water and drain them. Roll them in a little bechamel sauce. Break your eggs into the pan into which you have put a little butter; stir them with a fork in your left hand, adding salt and pepper with your right. This will only take a minute. Add the asparagus-tops in the thick sauce; this will take another minute. Roll or fold up the omelette and slip it on a hot buttered dish.

[*Mme. van Praet.*]

STUFFED EGGS

Hard-boil your eggs, allowing half an egg for each person. Take out the yolk. While they are boiling and afterwards cooling in water, make a small quantity of mayonnaise sauce. Peel the eggs, cut them through lengthways, and take out the yolks. Crumble these with a little chopped herbs, and add the mayonnaise. Fill the eggs with this mixture, and place them in a dish with chopped lettuce round it, to which you may add a little more of the sauce.

[*Mme. van Marcke de Lunessen.*]

POACHED EGGS, TOMATO SAUCE

Make some rounds of toast and butter them; place on each a slice of tongue or of ham. Keep these hot, and poach as many eggs as you require. Slip each egg on the toasts, and cover them quickly with a highly seasoned tomato sauce.

[*Mme. van Marcke de Lunessen.*]

EGGS AND MUSHROOMS

Pick over half a pound of mushrooms, cut them in small pieces like dice, and put them to stew in the oven with plenty of butter, pepper, and salt. Make a thick white sauce, and you may add to it the juice from the mushrooms when they are cooked; then stir in the mushrooms. Take three hard-boiled eggs, and separate yolks from whites. Put into a shallow vegetable-dish the whites cut up in small pieces, pour over them the bechamel with the mushrooms, and finish up by sprinkling over the top the hard-boiled yolks, which you have crumbled up with a fork.

[*Mme. Braconnière.*]

BELGIAN EGGS

Make some scrambled eggs, and place them on a very hot dish, and pour round them a thick tomato sauce. Decorate the dish quickly with thick rounds of tomato.

EGGS À LA RIBEAUCOURT

Butter some little paper cases, and let them dry in the oven. Put into each one a pat of butter and let it melt lightly. Break an egg into each case, taking care not to break the yolk, and put a bit of butter on each yolk. Place in a quick oven till the whites are half set. At the moment of serving take them out, and have ready some minced tongue or ham, to sprinkle on them, and decorate with a big bit of truffle.

TO USE UP REMAINS OF MEAT

Cut in slices the remains of any cold meat, such as pork, beef, veal, ham, or mutton. Melt in a pan a bit of salt butter the size of a walnut, and put in it an onion cut into fine slices; let it get brown in the hot butter. In another pan put a larger piece of butter rolled in a soup-spoonful of flour; add to it the onion and butter, and add enough water to prevent the sauce from getting very thick. Add, if you wish it, a teaspoonful of meat-extract and a pinch of salt. Have ready some mashed potatoes, but let them be very light. Place the slices of meat in a fireproof dish, pour the sauce on them, then the mashed potatoes, and put the dish in the oven, all well heated through. This is called in Belgium *"un philosophe. "*

[*Paquerette.*]

VEAL WITH ONIONS

Take a lump of butter the size of an egg, and let it color in a saucepan. Slice some onions and fry them in another pan. When fried, add them to the butter with some sliced carrots, a few small onions, and your pieces of veal, salt, and pepper. Add a small quantity of water, and close the lid on the saucepan. When the meat is tender, you can thicken the sauce with a little flour. This is a good way to use veal that is hard, or parts that are not the best cuts.

[*Paquerette.*]

VEAL CAKE

Mince very finely three pounds of raw veal and one-fourth pound of pork. It is better to do this at home than to have it done at the butcher's. Put two slices of bread to soak in milk, add two yolks of eggs and the whites, pepper and salt. Mix it well, working it for ten minutes. Then let it rest for half-an-hour. Put it in a small stewpan, add a lump of butter the size of a pigeon's egg, and put it in the oven. It will be ready to serve when the juice has ceased to run out.

[*Paquerette*]

TO USE UP COLD MEAT

Take a fresh celery, wash it well, and remove the green leaves. Let it boil till half-cooked in salted water. Drain it on a sieve, and then cut it lengthways, and place minced meat of any kind, well seasoned, between the two pieces. Tie them together with a thread and let them cook again for a quarter of an hour, this time either in the same water and gently simmered, or in the oven in a well-buttered dish. Other people, to avoid the trouble of tying the two halves, spread the mince on each half and cook it in the oven, laid flat in a fireproof dish. In this case put a good lump of butter on each portion of mince.

[*L. Verhaeghe.*]

FLEMISH CARBONADE

Put two onions to color in butter or in hot fat. Then add to them the beef, which you have cut into pieces the size of a small cake. Let it cook for a few minutes, then add pepper, salt, a carrot sliced, and enough water to allow the meat to cook gently by the side of the fire, allowing one and one-half hours for one and one-half pounds of meat. Ten minutes before serving add to the sauce a little meat-juice or Liebig. You may at the same time, if it is wished, cook potatoes with the meat for about twenty minutes. Serve it all in a large dish, the meat in the center and the potatoes round. The sauce is served separately, and without being passed through the sieve.

[*L. Verhaeghe.*]

A USE FOR COLD MUTTON

Cut the mutton into neat pieces, take away all fat and skin. Fry in butter and add all sorts of vegetables in dice, with thyme, bay-leaves, and parsley. Let all this stew very gently for two hours; you must add more stock or water to prevent it getting dry. Keep the lid of the pan on and, half-an-hour before serving, put in peeled potatoes. This dish is served very liquid.

[*Mme. Spinette.*]

FLEMISH CARBONADES

Take four pounds of beef—there is a cut near the neck that is suitable for this recipe. Cut the meat in small pieces (square) and fry them in a pan. In another pan put a piece of refined fat and fry in it five big onions that you have finely chopped. When these are well browned, add to them the meat, sprinkling in also pepper, salt, mixed herbs. Cover all with water, and let it cook for an hour with the lid on. After an hour's cooking, add half a glass of beer, a slice of crumb of bread with a light layer of mustard and three tablespoonfuls of best vinegar. Let it cook again for three quarters of an hour. If the sauce is not thick enough, add a little flour, taking care that it boils up again afterwards.

FISH

When there remains any cold fish, take away all skin and bones, mixing the flesh with salt, butter, pepper, and one or two raw eggs as you wish. Take some small fireproof cases and place in each some lemon-juice with a little melted butter and grated breadcrumbs. Bake the cases till the top of the fish is of a golden color.

REMAINS OF FISH

Make a good white sauce, add pepper, salt, and a little nutmeg and juice of a lemon. Add then your remains of fish and a few pickled shrimps. Fill some shells with it and sprinkle over the top a good powdering of grated Gruyère cheese. Lay a pat of butter in the middle of each shell and put them in the oven. When they are colored a good golden brown, serve them decorated with parsley.

[*Mme. Lekent.*]

GOOD RISSOLES

Mince any cold meat, adding to a pound of it one-half pound of fresh lean pork, a chopped shallot and parsley, salt, pepper, a little nutmeg, and bind with an egg, both yolk and white. Form into balls, and dip them in flour, then color them in some butter, and when they are nicely browned pour into the butter a little stock or meat-juice and water. Let them gently cook in it for ten minutes, and serve.

[*Mme. Lekent.*]

CROQUETTES OF BOILED MEAT

I think that boiled meat when cold is often neglected as being tasteless, but, prepared as I will show you, it will deserve your approval.

Mince your boiled meat and put it into a thick white sauce well-spiced with pepper, salt, and nutmeg, and let it remain for two hours. Then prepare your croquettes by rolling the mixture in white of egg and fine breadcrumbs. Put a piece of butter in the saucepan, sufficient to take all the croquettes, and let them brown in it for about ten minutes. A white sauce served with them is a good addition.

[*Mlle. A. Demeulemeester.*]

CARBONADES DONE WITH BEER

Cut the meat into slices that are thin rather than thick. Mince two big onions and fry them till brown; then fry the slices till they are colored on both sides. Pour on them first some beer, then a dash of vinegar, adding thyme, pepper, and salt, and throw in also a slice of crust of bread, which you have spread with mustard. Let this all simmer for three hours.

[*Mme. Segur.*]

WALLOON ENTRÉE

Make some toasted bread, either cut in rounds or in squares, and butter them. Cut some slices of salt beef, or, better still, ham, and put them on top; spread the meat with a good layer of grated cheese, and over that place another piece of buttered toast of corresponding shape. Melt some butter in a small saucepan and fry the rounds till they are golden-brown.

[*Mme. E. Maes.*]

SCRAPS OF MEAT

Your scraps of meat must be cut small or roughly minced; add to them a little sausage-meat, about a quarter as much, and a slice of white crumb bread that you have dipped in water or milk, and well drained. If eggs are not too dear, add two eggs, mixing them with the meat. Place the dish in the oven for half-an-hour—but it must be a slow oven—and take care that the meat does not become dry.

[*V. Verachtert.*]

FRICADELLE

For one pound of minced pork take one and one-half pounds of minced veal; cut three slices of white bread the thickness of nearly an inch, and crumble them up; two raw eggs, pepper and salt. Mix it all well, and place it in the oven for half-an-hour. If you eat this hot, serve it with a gravy sauce. If you wish for a supper-dish, put salad round the meat.

CHICORY AND HAM WITH CHEESE SAUCE

Cook the chicories gently in butter till they are done. Then take each one, and roll it in a slice of ham, and put them in a fireproof dish. Then make a very good white sauce of flour and butter and milk, adding cheese to flavor it strongly, and the yolk of an egg. Pour this sauce over the chicory, and place the dish in the oven. Let it turn brownish, and then serve it directly.

[*Mme. Vandervalle.*]

CROQUETTES OF VEAL

Make first of all a very thick white sauce of flour, milk, and butter, not forgetting also salt and pepper; when it is very thick add grated Gruyère cheese, in the proportion of a heaped teaspoonful of this to a breakfast-cupful of sauce. Take it off the fire, and stir in first of all the juice of a lemon, and then the yolk of an egg. Let it get cold. Then mince up finely your veal, or, indeed, any lean meat. Mix it well with the sauce, and make croquettes of it. Then roll each in the white of egg that you have left, and then in grated breadcrumbs, and fry in deep fat.

[*Mme. Vandervalle.*]

ENTRÉE (CROQUE-MONSIEUR)

Cut out some rounds of crumb of bread, of equal size, with a tin cutter; or, failing that, with a wine-glass. Butter all the rounds and sprinkle them with grated cheese—for preference with Gruyère. On half the number of rounds place a bit of ham cut to the same size. Put a lump of butter the weight of egg into a pan, and fry with the rounds in it, till they become golden. When they are a nice color, place one round dressed with cheese on a round dressed with ham, so as to have the golden bread both above and below. Serve them very hot, and garnished with fried parsley.

[*E. Defouck.*]

HOT-POT

Before putting in your meat, cook in the water a celery, four leeks, two onions, two turnips, two carrots; then add the meat, with pepper and salt, and stew gently for three hours. If you can put in a marrow-bone as well, that will give the soup a delicious flavor.

[*V. Verachtert.*]

HOCHE POT

One pound of fresh pork, one pound rump (flank) of beef, one pound rump of veal, two onions, one celery, four leeks, two or three carrots, two or three turnips, according to the size, a few Brussels sprouts, five or six potatoes, according to the number of persons. Let the water boil before putting in the meat, and cut all the vegetables in cubes of the same size, like cubes of sugar. Let simmer only, for three hours; it is delicious and makes a dinner.

[*V. Verachtert.*]

BOUCHÉES À LA REINE

Get some little cases from the pastry-cook of puff paste, which are to be filled with sweetbread cut in dice. It is a good plan to heat the cases before filling them.

The filling mixture. Cook the sweetbreads in water with pepper and salt, till done, skin them and cut in dice. Prepare a good bechamel sauce, seasoned with the juice of a lemon, and add to it a few mushrooms that have been fried in butter. Heat the dice of sweetbread in this sauce and fill the cases with it. Put them back in the oven to get quite hot.

HOCHE POT OF GHENT

Clean two big carrots and cut them into small pieces, the same for two turnips, four leeks, two celeries, and a good green cabbage, only using the pale leaves. Wash all these vegetables well in running water, two or three times, and put them on the fire in three and one-half pints of water. Add salt, and let it cook for an hour. At the end of this time, add a good piece of pork weighing perhaps three pounds—for choice let it be cutlets. You can also add a pig's trotter. Let it cook for another hour, taking care that the meat remains below the water. At the end of that time, and half-an-hour before you wish to eat it, add potatoes enough to be three for each person. Watch the cooking so as to see that the potatoes do not stick, and finish the seasoning with pepper and salt.

[*Georges Kerckaert.*]

CARBONADE OF FLANDERS

Cut your beef into small neat pieces. Mince some onions finely, and for five or six people you would add two bay-leaves, two cloves, pepper, salt; simmer gently for three hours in water, and at the end of that time bind the sauce with cornflour. Some people like the sauce to be thickened instead with mustard.

[*V. Verachtert.*]

HEADLESS SPARROWS

Take two pounds of beef, which must be lean and cut in thin slices. Cut your slices of beef in pieces of five inches by three. Put in the middle of each piece a little square of very fat bacon, a sprig of parsley, pepper and salt. Roll up the slices and tie them round with a thread so that the seasoning remains inside. Melt in a pan a lump of butter the size of a very big egg. Let it get brown and then, after rolling the beef in flour, put them in the butter. Let them cook thus for five minutes, add half a pint of water, and let them simmer for two hours. Fill up with water if it becomes too dry. Before serving, take great care to remove the threads.

[*A Belgian at Droitwich.*]

MUTTON STEW

Take two pounds of mutton, the breast or one of the inferior parts will do as well as a prime piece. Put in an earthenware pan a lump of butter as big as an egg, and let it color. Cut the mutton in pieces and let them color in the butter, adding salt and pepper, a few onions or shallots. When all is colored, add at least a pound of turnips, cut in slices, with about a pint of water. Let it boil up till the turnips are tender. Then add two and one-half or three pounds of potatoes; salt and pepper these, but in moderation, if the meat has been already salted and peppered. Add some thyme and bay-leaves, and let them all cook very gently till the potatoes are tender. When these are cooked, take out the pieces of meat, mix the turnips and potatoes, so as to make a uniform mixture; then place the meat on the top of the mixture, and serve it. N. B. It is necessary to watch the cooking of this dish very carefully, so that you can add a little water whenever it becomes necessary, for if one leaves the preparation a little too dry it quickly burns.

[*A Belgian at Droitwich.*]

HOCHE POT GANTOIS

(For eight or nine persons)

Take one pound beef, one pound salt pork, and one pound mutton; cut into pieces about three inches by two, let it boil, and skim. Take two or three carrots, one large turnip, one large head of celery, three or four leeks, a good green cabbage, cut in four, the other vegetables cut into pieces of moderate size, not too small; put them in with the meat, and see that they are first covered by the water. Let it boil for three to four hours, and three quarters of an hour before dishing, add some potatoes cut in pieces.

To dish: Place the meat in the center of a flat dish, and the vegetables around; serve the liquid in a soup-tureen. This dish should be eaten out of soup plates, as it is soup and meat course at one time.

CHINESE CORKS

Make a thick white sauce, and when it has grown a little cold, add the yolk of one egg, and a few drops of lemon-juice. Sprinkle in a slice of stale bread, and enough grated cheese to flavor it strongly, and leave it to cool for two hours. Then shape into small pieces like corks, dip them into the beaten whites of your egg, and then into grated breadcrumbs. Have ready some hot fat, or lard, and fry the cheese-balls in it till they are golden.

[*Mme. Limpens.*]

LIMPENS CHEESE

Take a roll and, cutting it in slices, remove the crusts so that a round of crumbs remain. Butter each slice, and cover it well with grated cheese, building up the slices one on the top of the other. Boil a cupful of milk, with pepper, salt, and a little nutmeg; when boiled, pour it over the bread till it is well soaked. Put them in the oven, for quarter of an hour, according to the heat of the oven and the quantity you have. You must pour its juice over it every now and then, and when the top is turning into a crust, serve it.

[*Mme. Limpens.*]

CHEESE SOUFFLÉ

Take two good soup-spoonfuls of flour, and mix it with half a teacupful of milk; melt a lump of butter, the size of a filbert, and add that, then enough grated cheese to your taste, and the yolks of four eggs. Add at the last the whites of the four eggs, beaten stiffly; pepper and salt. Butter a mold, put in your mixture, and let it cook for one hour in a saucepan, surrounded with boiling water, and the lid on. Then turn out the soufflé, and serve with a mushroom sauce. The sauce is a good white sauce, to which you add already cooked mushrooms. Clean them first of all, chop them, and cook them till tender in butter; and their own juice; then throw them into the sauce, and pour it over your soufflé.

[*Mme. Vandervalle.*]

CHEESE CROQUETTES

Make a thick bechamel sauce, and be sure that you cook it for ten minutes, constantly stirring. Add, till well flavored, some Gruyère and Parmesan cheese, mixed and grated. Let it all get cold. Then roll this mixture into the shape of carrots; roll them in finely-grated breadcrumbs, and fry them in hot lard or refined fat. Lay them on a hot dish, and, at the thicker end of each carrot stick in a sprig of parsley to look like the stalk.

[*Mme. van Marcke de Lunessen.*]

CHEESE FONDANTS

For twelve fondants make a white sauce with two soupspoons of flour and milk. Add to it the yolks of three eggs. Stir in four ounces of mixed Gruyère cheese, and Parmesan, grated very finely. Add at the end the juice of half a lemon, and a dust of cayenne. Let it all grow cold. Then make little balls with this paste and roll them in breadcrumbs. Throw them in a pan of boiling fat, where they must remain till they are a good golden color. Drain them, keeping them hot, and serve quickly.

[*Madame Emelie Jones*]

CHEESE SOUFFLÉ

Grate half a pound of Gruyère cheese. Mix in a cup of milk a dessert-spoonful of flour; beat four whole eggs, and add first the cheese, and then the flour and milk mixture. Season with pepper and salt, and put all into a mold. Let it cook in a saucepan of boiling water for an hour and a half. Then at the end of this time put it in the oven for half an hour.

[*Madame Emelie Jones.*]

POTATOES AND CHEESE

Wash some raw potatoes, peel them, cut them into very thin round slices. Take a dish which will stand the oven, and be nice enough to go on the table, and put in it a layer of the slices sprinkled with pepper, salt, a little flour, and plenty of grated Gruyère. Continue in this way, finishing with a layer of cheese, and a little flour. Put the dish in the oven, which must not be a very hot one, and cook gently.

For a medium pie dish you will find that half an hour will be sufficient to cook the potatoes.

[*Madame Emelie Jones.*]

YORK HAM, SWEETBREADS, MADEIRA SAUCE

Heat the ham in a double saucepan (bain marie). Boil the sweetbreads, blanch them and let them fry in some butter.

Take flour and butter and melt them to a thick sauce, adding a tumbler of water and Liebig which will turn your sauce brown. Fry half a pound of mushrooms in butter and when brown, add them and the liquor to your sauce with a good glass of madeira or sherry. Place your ham in the middle of the dish, surround it with the sweetbreads, and pour over all the Madeira sauce.

[*Mme. Vandervalle.*]

HAM WITH MADEIRA SAUCE

Cook some macaroni or spaghetti, with salt and pepper. Make a brown sauce, using plenty of butter, for this dish requires a great deal of sauce, and add to your "roux" some tomatoes in purée (stewed and run through a sieve), a little meat extract, some fried mushrooms, a few drops of good brandy or madeira to your taste. Let your slices of ham heat in this sauce, and when ready, place them in the middle of a flat dish, put the mushrooms or spaghetti round, and put the sauce, very hot, over the ham.

[*Madame Spinette.*]

A DIFFICULT DISH OF EGGS

And yet this is only fried eggs after all! Put some oil on to heat; if you have not oil use butter, but oil is the best. When the bluish steam rises it is hot enough. Break an egg into a little flat dish, tip up the frying pan at the handle side, and slip the egg into it, then with a wooden spoon turn the egg over on itself; that is, roll the white of it over the yolk as it slips into the pan. If you cannot manage this, let the egg heat for a second, and then roll the white over the yolk with a wooden spoon. Do each egg in this way, and as soon as one is done let it drain and keep warm by the fire. When all are done put them in a circle, in a dish, and pour round them a very hot sauce, either made with tomatoes, or flavored with vinegar and mustard.

COUNTRY EGGS

Make a white sauce thickly mixed with onions, such as you would eat in England with a leg of mutton, but do not forget a little seasoning of mace. Make a high mold of mashed potatoes, and then scoop it out from the top, leaving the bottom and high sides of the vegetable. While your sauce is kept by the fire (the potatoes also), boil six eggs for two minutes, shell them, and you will find the whites just set and no more. Pour the onion sauce into the potato, and drop in the whole eggs and serve very hot.

FRENCH EGGS

Put a lump of butter the size of an egg in a fireproof dish, mixing in when it is melted some breadcrumbs, a chopped leek, the inside of three tomatoes, pepper and salt. Let it cook for three or four minutes in the oven, then stir in the yolks of two eggs, and let it make a custard.

Then break on the top of this custard as many eggs as you wish; sprinkle with pepper and salt. Let it remain in the oven till these last are beginning to set. Take out the dish, and pass over the top the salamander, or the shovel, red hot, and serve at once. I have seen this dish with the two extra whites of eggs beaten and placed in a pile on the top, and slightly browned by the shovel.

OEUFS CELESTES

(Hommage à Sir Edward Grey)

Gently boil a quantity of the very best green peas in good gravy; as the gravy becomes reduced, add, instead, butter. Do not forget to have put a lump of sugar in every pint of gravy. When the peas are done break on them the required number of fresh eggs, with pepper and salt. Place all in a double saucepan, till the eggs are just done. It is a pity that in England there are no cooking pots made, which will hold fire on the top, so that a dish, such as this, becomes easily done in a few minutes.

PETITES CAISSES À LA FURNES

Take a small Ostend rabbit, steep it in water as usual, and boil it gently in some white stock, with a good many peppercorns. When it is cold chop the meat up into small dice; add to it about a quarter of the amount of ham, and the whites of two hard-boiled eggs, all cut to the same size.

Moisten the salpicon with a good white sauce made with cream, a little lemon juice, pepper and salt.

The little paper cases must have a ring of cress arranged, about a quarter of an inch thick; the salpicon, put in carefully with a small spoon, will hold it in place.

Fill the cases to the level of the cress leaves, and decorate with a Belgian flag made as follows:

Make some aspic jelly with gelatine, tarragon vinegar, and a little sherry. Color one portion with paprika or coralline, pepper; a second part with the sieved yolks of two hard-boiled eggs, and the remainder with rinsed pickled walnuts, also passed through a wire sieve. Pour the red jelly into a small mold with straight sides; when it is almost set pour in the yellow aspic, and when that is cold pour in the black. When the jelly is quite cold, turn it out, slice it, and cut it into pieces of suitable size. If you make too much aspic it can decorate any cold dish or salad. The walnut squash looks black at night.

[*Margaret Strail, or Mrs. A. Stuart.*]

FLEMISH CARROTS

Take some young carrots, wash and brush them as tenderly as you would an infant, then simmer them till tender in with pepper and salt. When cooked, draw them to the side of the fire and pour in some cream to make a good sauce. If you cannot use cream, take milk instead and stir with it the yolk of an egg. To thicken for use, add a pinch of sugar and some chopped parsley.

AUBERGINE OR EGG PLANT

This purple fruit is, like the tomato, always cooked as a vegetable. It is like the brinjal of the East. It is hardly necessary to give special recipes for the dressing of aubergines, for you can see their possibilities at a glance. They can be stuffed with white mince in a white sauce, when you would cut the fruit in half, remove some of the interior, fill up with mince and sauce, replace the top, and bake for twenty minutes, or simply cut in halves and stewed in stock, with pepper and salt they are good, or you can simmer them gently in water and when ready to serve, pour over them a white sauce as for vegetable marrow. If they are cheap in England the following entrée would be inexpensive and would look nice.

EGG PLANTS AS SOUFFLÉ

Wash the fruit, cut them lengthways, remove the inside. Fill each half with a mixture made of beaten egg, grated cheese, and some fine breadcrumbs, and a dash of mustard. Put the halves to bake for a quarter of an hour, or till the soufflé mixture has risen. When cooked place them in an oval dish with a border of rice turned out from a border mold.

POTATO CROQUETTES

Cook your potatoes, rub them through the sieve, add pepper and salt, two or three eggs, lightly beaten, mixing both yolks and whites, and according to the quantity you are making a little butter and milk. Work all well and let it get cold. Roll into croquettes, roll each in beaten egg, then in finely grated breadcrumbs, and let them cook in boiling fat or lard.

[*Madame Emelie Jones.*]

PURÉE OF CHESTNUTS

Make a little slit in each chestnut, boil them till tender, then put them in another pan with cold water in it and replace them on the fire. Peel them one by one as you take them out, and rub them through a sieve, pounding them first to make it easier, add salt, a good lump of butter and a little milk to make a nice purée. This is very good to surround grilled chicken or turkey legs, or for a salmi of duck or hare.

HORS D'OEUVRES

The attractive "savory" of English dinner tables finds its counterpart apparently in egg and fish dishes served cold at the beginning of a meal, and therefore what we should call hors d'oeuvres.

POTATO DICE

Boil your potatoes and let them be of the firm, soapy kind, not the floury kind. When cooked, and cold, cut them into dice, and toss them in the following sauce:

Take equal quantities of salad oil and cream, a quarter of that amount of tarragon vinegar, a pinch of salt, and a few chopped capers. Mix very well, and pour it on the dice. You may vary this by using cream only, in which case omit the vinegar. Season with pepper, salt, celery seed, and instead of the capers take some pickled nasturtium seed, and let that, finely minced, remain in the sauce for an hour before using it.

ANCHOVIES

Fillets of these, put in a lattice work across mashed potato look very nice. Be sure you use good anchovies preserved in salt, and well washed and soaked to take away the greater part of the saltness; or, if you can make some toast butter it when cold, cut it into thin strips, and lay a fillet in the center. Fill up the sides of the toast with chopped hard- boiled yolk of egg.

ANCHOVY SANDWICHES

Cut some bread and butter, very thin, and in fingers. Chop some water- cress, lay it on a finger, sprinkle a little Tarragon vinegar and water (equal quantities) over it, and then lay on a fillet of anchovy, cover with more cress and a finger of bread and butter. Put them in a pile under a plate to flatten and before serving trim the edges.

ANCHOVY ROUNDS

Make some toast, cut it in rounds, butter it when cold. Curl an anchovy round a stewed olive, and put it on the toast. Make a little border of yolk of egg boiled and chopped.

ANCHOVY BISCUITS

Made as you would make cheese biscuits, but using anchovy sauce instead to flavor them. If you make the pastry thin you can put some lettuce between two biscuits and press together with a little butter spread inside.

ANCHOVY PATTIES

Make some paste and roll it out thinly. Take a coffee cup and turning it upside down stamp out some rounds. Turn the cup the right way again, and put it on a round. Then you will see an edge of paste protruding all round. Turn this up with the end of a fork, which makes a pretty little edge. Do this with all, and fill the shallow cases then made with a good mayonnaise sauce in which you have put chopped celery and potato, and a small quantity of chopped gherkins. Lay three fillets of anchovy across each other to form a six-pointed star and season highly with cayenne pepper.

All the above recipes can be followed using sardines instead of anchovies, and indeed one can use them in many other ways, with eggs, with lettuce, with tomatoes. As anchovies are rather expensive to buy, I give a recipe for mock anchovies, which is easy to do, but it must be done six months before using the fish.

MOCK ANCHOVIES

When sprats are cheap, buy a good quantity, what in England you would call a peck. Do not either wipe or wash them. Take four ounces of saltpeter, a pound of bay salt, two pounds of common coarse salt, and pound them well, then add a little cochineal to color it, pound and mix very well. Take a stone jar and put in it a layer of the mixture and a layer of the sprats, on each layer of fish adding three or four bay leaves and a few whole pepper-corns. Fill up the jar and press it all down very firmly. Cover with a stone cover, and let them stand for six months before you use them.

CUCUMBER À LA LAEKEN

Take a cucumber and cut it in pieces two inches long, then peel away the dark green skin for one inch, leaving the other inch as it was. Set up each piece on end, scoop it out till nearly the bottom and fill up with bits of cold salmon or lobster in mayonnaise sauce. Cold turbot or any other delicate fish will do equally well or a small turret of whipped cream, slightly salted, should be piled on top. This dish never fails to please.

HERRING AND MAYONNAISE

Take some salt herring, a half for each person, and soak them for a day in water. Skin them, cut them open lengthwise, take out the backbone, and put them to soak in vinegar. Then before serving them let them lie for a few minutes in milk, and putting them on a dish pour over them a good mayonnaise sauce. [*Mlle. Oclhaye.*]

SWEET DRINKS AND CORDIALS. ORGEAT

Blanch first of all half a pound of sweet almonds and three ounces of bitter, turn them into cold water for a few minutes; then you must pound them very fine in a stone mortar, if you have a marble one so much the better, and do it in a cool place.

You must add a little milk occasionally to prevent the paste from becoming oily, then add three quarts of fresh milk, stirring it in slowly, sweeten to your taste, and then putting all into a saucepan clean as a chalice, bring it to the boil.

Boil for ten minutes, and then stir till cold, strain it through finest muslin, and then add two good glasses of brandy. Bottle and keep in a dark place.

HAWTHORN CORDIAL

When the hawthorn is in full bloom, pick a basketful of the blooms. Take them home, and put the white petals into a large glass bottle, taking care that you put in no leaves or stalks. When the bottle is filled to the top do not press it down, but pour in gently as much good French Brandy as it will hold. Cork and let it stand for three months, then you can strain it off. This is good as a cordial, and if you find it too strong, add water, or sweeten it with sugar.

DUTCH NOYEAU

Peel finely the rinds of five large lemons, or of six small ones, then throw on it a pound of loaf sugar that you have freshly pounded, two ounces of bitter almonds, chopped and pounded; mix these with two quarts of the best Schnappes or Hollands, and add six tablespoonfuls of boiling milk.

Fill your jars with this, cover it close, and put it in a passage or hall, where people can shake it every day.

Leave it there for three weeks, and strain it through some blotting paper into another bottle. It will be ready to drink.

LAVENDER WATER

Take a large bottle, and put in it twelve ounces of the best spirits of wine, one essence of ambergris, twopennyworth of musk, and three drachms of oil of lavender.

Cork it tightly, put in a dark place, and shake it every day for a month. This is really lavender spirit, as no water is used.

HOT BURGUNDY

Take half a pint of good Burgundy wine, put it to boil with two cloves, and a dust of mixed spice, sweeten to taste with some powdered sugar. If you like add a quarter of the quantity of water to the wine before boiling.

CRÊME DE POISSON À LA ROI ALBERT

Take a fresh raw whiting, fillet it, and pass the flesh through a wire sieve.

For a small dish take four ounces of the fish, mix them lightly with four tablespoonfuls of very thick cream, adding pepper and salt. Fill an oval ring mold, and steam gently for twenty minutes, under buttered paper.

Have some marine crayfish boiled, shell the tails, cut them in pieces, removing the black line inside. Cut three truffles into thick slices, heat them and the crayfish in some ordinary white sauce, enriched with the yolk of a raw egg, pepper and salt, and one dessertspoonful of tarragon vinegar. This must not be allowed to boil. When the cream is turned out into a hot silver dish, pour the ragout into the center, and put a hot lid on.

This dish, and that on page 86-87, has been composed by a Scotch lady in honor of the King of the Belgians. Not every cook can manage the cream, but the proportions are exact, and so is the time.

[*Mrs. Alex. Stuart.*]

FISH AND CUSTARD

Boil up the trimmings of your fish with milk, pepper and salt. Strain it and add the yolks of eggs till you get a good custard. Pour the custard into a mold, and lay in it your fish, which must already be parboiled. If you have cold fish, flake it, and mix it with the custard. Put the mold in a double saucepan. Steam it for three quarters of an hour. Turn it out, and garnish with strips of lemon peel, and if you have it, sprigs of fennel.

HAKE AND POTATOES

Hake, which is not one of the most delicate fish, can be made excellent if stewed in the following sauce: A quart of milk to which you have added a dessertspoonful of any of the good English sauces; thicken it with a knob of butter rolled in flour, which stir in till all is smooth. When it boils take off the fire, and put in your pieces of hake, set it back by the side of the fire to keep very hot, without boiling, for twenty-five minutes. Meanwhile mash some potatoes, and put it as a purée round a dish, pour the fish in the center, sprinkle on it chopped parsley. The liquor ought to be much reduced.

VERY NICE SKATE

Take skate, or indeed any fish that rolls up easily, make into fillets, dry them well, and sprinkle on each fillet, pepper, salt, a dust of mixed spice, and chopped parsley. Roll each fillet up tightly, and pack them tightly into a dish, so that they will not become loose. Take vinegar and beer in equal quantities, or, if you do not like to use beer, you must add to the vinegar some whole black pepper, and a good sprinkle of dried and mixed herbs with salt. Pour over the fish, tie a piece of buttered paper over the top, and bake for an hour and a quarter (for a medium pie dish) in a moderate oven.

TO KEEP SPRATS

A large quantity of these may be bought cheaply and kept for some weeks by this method. Put on to warm equal quantities of vinegar and water, what you think sufficient to cover your sprats, allowing for wastage; and stir in for every quart of liquor a small saltspoonful of mixed spice, four bay leaves, a shallot minced, a small bunch of bruised thyme, the thin rind of a half lemon, salt and pepper; if you can use tarragon vinegar so much the better. Clean the sprats, remove tails and heads, and lay them in a deep dish. Take your liquor and pour it over the fish, tie a large paper over all, and let them bake in a cool oven for two or three hours; or cook them in a double saucepan; in any case do them very slowly. Put aside to cool, and take out the fish to use as required. They will keep good four weeks.

TO KEEP MACKEREL FOR A WEEK

It sometimes happens that you can get a great quantity of this fish, very fresh, cheaply, and wish to use it later on.

Pickle it thus: Boil a pint of vinegar with six peppercorns, four cloves, four bay leaves, a scrap of mace, a saltspoonful of salt, and the same of made mustard. When this is boiled up put it to cool. Lay your mackerel prepared ready for eating, and sprinkle on each piece some salt, and minced thyme. It may be an hour before using.

Then fry the fish, lifting each piece carefully into the hot fat. When fried lay the fish in a deep dish, and pour on each piece your vinegar liquor till all is covered.

Cover over with paper such as you use for jam pots, well tied down. You can afterwards heat the fish as you require.

A BROWN DISH OF FISH

Take your fish, which should be herring or mackerel, relieve it of the bones, skin and fins, which you must put to boil for three quarters of an hour in water, with pepper and salt. After that time strain off the liquor, and add to it enough browning to color it well.

Then brown quarter of a pound of butter and knead into it two tablespoonfuls of flour, add it, when well mixed, to your liquor, with salt and pepper, a piece of lemon peel, and a dust of mixed spice. Bring all this to the boil and drop in your fish. (Cut in neat fillets.) Let them simmer for twenty minutes, and if too dry pour in some darkly colored gravy. Just before you wish to serve add a good wine glass of claret, or of Burgundy, take out the lemon peel, and pour all on a hot dish. If you do not wish to put wine, the flavor of the sauce is very excellent if you stir into it a dessertspoonful of mushroom ketchup, or a teaspoonful of soy. This brown fish is nice to follow a white soup.

BAKED HADDOCKS

Take all the trimmings of two good sized haddocks, cover them with milk and water, and put them to simmer. Add chopped parsley, a chopped shallot, pepper and salt.

Cut each fish in half across, and lay them in the bottom of a pie dish, sprinkle breadcrumbs, pats of butter, pepper and salt, between and on each piece. Fill up the dish with water or milk, adding the simmered and strained liquor from the trimmings.

Bake gently for an hour, and when brown on top add more breadcrumbs, and pats of butter.

FILLETED SOLES AU FROMAGE

Boil the filleted soles in water. Make a sauce with butter. One spoonful of flour—milk, pepper and salt, powdered cheese (Cheddar). Boil it, adding some washed and chopped mushrooms and a little cream. Put the filets on a dish and pour them over the sauce. Leave it about a quarter of an hour in the oven, so that it becomes slightly browned.

[*Mdlle. Spreakers.*]

FILLETED FISH, WITH WHITE SAUCE AND TOMATOES

Brown two onions in butter, and add a spray of parsley, half a pound of tomatoes and a claret glassful of white wine. Let this simmer for half an hour, and then pass it through the tammy. Then fry half a pound of mushrooms, and add them and their liquor to the sauce, thickening it, if necessary, with a little cornflour. A great improvement is a little liebig. Place your fish in the oven, and cook it gently in butter, with pepper and salt. When it is done, serve it with the sauce poured over it.

[*Madame Vandervalle.*]

THE MILLER'S COD

(Cabillaud meunier)

Cut your cod in slices, and roll them in flour. Put them to fry in a good piece of butter, adding chopped parsley, pepper and salt, and the juice of one lemon. This is very good, if served in the dish that it is cooked in.

DUTCH HERRINGS

(A cold dish)

Take some Dutch, or some salted herrings, and remove the skin, backbones, etc. Lay the fish in milk for at least twenty-four hours to get the salt out. Make a mayonnaise sauce, adding to it the roe from the herrings, in small pieces; wipe and drain the fish, and pour over them the sauce.

REMAINS OF COD

I

Take your fish, and remove all bones and skin. Put some butter to brown in a saucepan, and when it is colored, add the cod, sprinkling in pepper and salt and a good thickening of grated breadcrumbs. Let this all heat gently by the fire and turn it into paper cases, with chopped parsley on the top.

II

The above recipe can be followed for making fish rissoles, but, after having mixed it well, let it grow cold. Then form into balls, roll them in breadcrumbs, and throw them into boiling fat.

III

Take all the remains of the fish and heat them in butter. Make some mashed potatoes, and add to them some white sauce, made of flour, milk and butter. Mix this with the fish, so that it is quite moist, and do not forget salt and pepper. Place the mixture in a fireproof dish and sprinkle breadcrumbs over it. Bake for fifteen minutes, or till it is hot through, and serve as it is.

[*Mdlle. M. Schmidt, of Antwerp.*]

* * * * *

PART II

The second half of this little book is composed chiefly of recipes for dishes that can be made in haste, and by the inexperienced cook. But such cook can hardly pay too much attention to details if she does not wish to revert to an early, not to say feral type of cuisine, where the roots were eaten raw while the meat was burnt. Because your dining-room furniture is Early English, there is no reason why the cooking should be early English too. And it certainly will be, unless one takes great trouble with detail.

Let us suppose that at 7:30 P. M. your husband telephones that he is bringing a friend to dine at 8. Let us suppose an even more rash act. He arrives at 7:15, he brings a friend: you perceive the unexpressed corollary that the dinner must be better than usual. In such a moment of poignant surprise, let fly your best smile (the kind that is practiced by bachelors' widows) and say "I am delighted you have come like this; do you mind eight or a quarter past for dinner? " Then melt away to the cook with this very book in your hand.

I take it that you consider her to be the junior partner in the household, you, of course, being the senior, and your husband the sleeping partner in it. Ask what there is in the house for an extra dish, and I wager you the whole solar system to a burnt match that you will find in these pages the very recipe that fits the case. A piece of cold veal, viewed with an eye to futurity, resolves itself into a white creamy delightfulness that melts in your mouth; a new-laid egg, maybe, poached on the top, and all set in a china shell. If you have no meat at all, you must simply hoodwink your friends with the fish and vegetables.

You know the story of the great Frenchwoman:

"Hèlas, Annette, I have some gentlemen coming to dine, and we have no meat in the house. What to do? "

"Ah! Madame, I will cook at my best; and if Madame will talk at her best, they will never notice there is anything wrong. "

But for the present day, I would recommend rather that the gentlemen be beguiled into doing the talking themselves, if any shortcoming in the menu is to be concealed from them, for then their attention will be engaged.

It takes away from the made-in-a-hurry look of a dish if it is decorated, and there are plenty of motifs in that way besides parsley. One can use beetroot, radishes, carrots cut in dice, minced pickles, sieved egg; and for sweets, besides the usual preserved cherries and angelica, you can have strips of lemon peel, almonds pointed or chopped, stoned prunes cut in halves, wild strawberries, portions of tangerine orange. There is a saying,

> Polish the shoe,
> Though the sole be through,

and a very simple chocolate shape may be made attractive by being garnished with a cluster of pointed almonds in the center, surrounded by a ring of tangerine pieces, well skinned and laid like many crescents one after the other. There is nothing so small and insignificant but has great possibilities. Did not Darwin raise eighty seedlings from a single clod of earth taken from a bird's foot?

It is to be regretted that Samuel Johnson never wrote the manual that he contemplated. "Sir, " he said, "I could write a better book of cookery than has ever yet been written. It should be a book on philosophical principles. "

Perhaps the pies of Fleet Street reminded him of the Black Broth of the Spartans which the well-fed Dionysius found excessively nasty; the tyrant was curtly told that it was nothing indeed without the seasoning of fatigue and hunger. We do not wish a meal to owe its relish solely to the influence of extreme hunger—it must have a beautiful nature all its own, it must exhibit the idea of Thing-in-Itself in an easily assimilable form.

I am convinced, anyhow, that this little collection (formed through the kindness of our Belgian friends) will work miracles; for there are plenty of miracles worked nowadays, though not by those romantic souls who think that things come by themselves. Good dinners certainly do not, and I end with this couplet:

> A douce woman and a fu' wame
> Maks King and cottar bide at hame.

Which, being interpreted, means that if you want a man to stay at home, you must agree with him and so must his dinner.

M. LUCK.

HORS D'OEUVRE

(Herring and Mayonnaise)

Take some salt herrings, one for each person, and soak them for a day in water. Skin them, cut them open lengthways, take out the backbone, and put them to soak for a day in vinegar. Then before serving them, let them lie for a few minutes in milk, and, putting them on a dish, pour over them a good mayonnaise sauce.

[*Mme. Delhaye.*]

CARROT SOUP

Wash and scrape a pound of carrots, slice them, treat two medium sized potatoes in the same manner, add a bay leaf, a sprig of thyme and a chopped onion. Cook all with water, add salt, pepper, and cook gently till tender, when pass it through a sieve. Put in a pan a lump of butter the size of an egg, with a chopped leek and a sprig of chervil. Let it cook gently for three or four minutes, then pour on the puree of carrots and let it all come to the boil before taking it off to serve.

[*Madame Stoppers.*]

SORREL SOUP

Take a quart of bouillon or of meat extract and water. Fry in butter a carrot, a turnip, an onion, a small cabbage, all washed and chopped, and add half a teaspoonful of castor sugar. Put your soup to it and set on the fire. Let it simmer for twenty minutes, add any seasoning you wish and a little more water, and let it simmer for another half hour. Then shred a bit of basil or marjoram with a handful of well washed sorrel, throw them in, cook for five minutes, skim it, pour it into a soup tureen, and serve.

OSTEND SOUP

There are many varieties of this soup to be met with in the different hotels, but it is a white soup, made of fish pieces and trimmings, strained, returned to the pot, and with plenty of cream and oysters added before serving. It should never boil after the cream is put in. A little mace is usual, but no onions or shallot. A simple variety is made with flour and milk instead of cream, the liquor of the oysters as well as the oysters, and a beaten egg added at the last moment.

[*Esperance.*]

ANOTHER SORREL SOUP

Take a tablespoonful of breadcrumbs, moisten them in milk in a pan, then add as much water as you require. Throw in three medium potatoes, a handful of well washed sorrel, and a sprig or two of chervil, a lump of butter, pepper, and salt. Bring to the boil, simmer for quarter of an hour, pass through a tammy, heat again for ten minutes and serve burning hot.

[*Esperance.*]

HASTY SOUP

Into a quart of boiling water throw lightly four tablespoonfuls of semolina, so that the grains are separated. Let it boil for a quarter of an hour, with pepper and salt. Take the tureen and put the yolk of an egg in it with a bit of butter the same size, mix them with a fork and pour in a teacupful of hot water with extract of meat in it, as strong as you wish. Quickly pour in the semolina soup and serve it at once. This is a quickly made and inexpensive dish, besides which it is a nice one.

[*Madame Alphonse F.*]

ARTICHOKES A LA VEDETTE

Boil some globe artichokes in salted water till they are tender. Take out the center leaves, leaving an even fringe of leaves on the outside. Remove as much of the choke as you can. Put them back in a steamer. Toss some cooked peas in butter, then mix them in cream and taking up your artichokes again put in your cream and peas in the center of each, as much as you can get in. The cream is not necessary for this dish to be a good one, but the artichokes and peas must both be young. As a rule people cut their fruit too soon and their vegetables too late.

[*Chef reconnaissant.*]

SURPRISE POTATOES

Quarter of an hour will suffice to prepare and cook this savory surprise, once the potatoes are baked. Take three large potatoes of symmetrical size, clean and bake them; cut each in two and remove the inside without injuring the skin. Melt half an ounce of butter by the fire, add two ounces of potato passed through a sieve, a teaspoonful of grated parmesan, pepper, salt, and a tablespoonful of milk. Then stir in the yolk of an egg and presently the white, well beaten. Fill the empty potato skins with the mixture which ought to rise and puff out in ten or twelve minutes.

VEGETABLE SALADS

Sometimes one has a few leeks, a half cauliflower, a handful each of peas and beans. Instead of currying these vegetables (which removes all distinctive flavor from them) cook them gently, and toss them when cold in a good salad dressing. If you can give the yolk of an egg to it, so much the better. Any cold meat is improved by a side dish of this sort. The vegetables that one can curry with advantage are large marrows, cut into cubes, turnips, potatoes, parsnips.

[*Marguerite Leblanc.*]

TOMATOES A LA SIR EDWARD GREY HOMMAGE

Take some fine firm tomatoes, not very ripe. Turn them with the stalk side up and cut a slice off the top with a sharp knife. Take out the inside with a teaspoon. Break into each tomato a pullet's egg, sprinkle with pepper and salt. The inside of the tomato you will pass through a fine wire sieve and it will be a thick liquor; mix it with bread-crumbs, salt, pepper, and some grated cheese till quite thick. Put this mixture on the top of each egg and place all in the oven for three or four minutes, so that the eggs are only just set and no more.

[*Amie inconnue.*]

STUFFED CARROTS

Take some good sized carrots, and after washing them well and cutting off the green tuft, cut each one across about two and a half inches from the leaves. Scoop out the inside yellow part, leaving a case of the redder part and a piece to form the bottom, at the smaller end. Then stew the cases very gently till a little tender, but not quite soft. Take them out of the water, drain them, and then placing each on its small end, fill up with hot chopped mushrooms, that have been tossed in butter. Arrange in a circle on a dish, and garnish with small sprigs of carrot leaves. The insides that you have scooped out are to be used for soup flavoring.

[*Pour la Patrie.*]

TO COOK ASPARAGUS

One should not let the tips of this vegetable touch the water. Take your bundle, dip the stalks in warm water to remove any dust, and the tips also, if it is necessary. Then tie the bundle round with tape, keeping the ends of stalks even so that it will stand upright. Place them in boiling water with the heads just sticking out, and keep them like that. In this way the heads, which are very tender, will be cooked in the steam and will not drop off.

[*Pour la Patrie.*]

TOMATOES IN HASTE

Butter a pie-dish, preferably a fireproof china dish. Open a tin of tomatoes and remove as much skin as you can if they are the unpeeled kind. Put a handful of crumbled brown bread in the dish with lumps of butter, then pour on that some tomatoes, dust with pepper and salt, then more bread, and so on, finishing at the last with lumps of butter, and a thick sprinkling of grated cheese. Bake for twenty minutes.

[*Pour la Patrie.*]

KIDNEYS AND LETTUCE

Put on some water to boil. Take your lettuce, and choose the round kind, and wash it well. Take out neatly with your fingers the center leaves, and fill up instead with a sheep's kidney which you have lightly dusted with flour, pepper, and salt. Tie the lettuce round very firmly and set it in a pan of boiling water that covers up only three quarters of the vegetable. Boil for eighteen minutes. Take out the lettuce, untie it, drain it, and serve at once. Kidneys are good when they are placed inside large Spanish onions and gently stewed, in which case a dab of made mustard is given them.

TOMATO RICE

Put on your rice to boil. Make a tomato sauce by stewing them gently, and then rubbing them through a sieve; this makes a purée, which you must put back to heat with pepper and salt and a small quantity of made mustard. Then grate some parmesan, or failing that, some Gruyère cheese. Take off the rice, drain it, keeping it hot, put it on a dish and pour over it your purée. Then sprinkle the grated cheese thickly on top of all.

[*Pour la Patrie.*]

RICE WITH EGGS

Boil some rice till it will press closely together. Fill some teacups with it, pressing the rice well down; then leave a hole in the middle and pour into each hole a small raw egg, yolk, and white. Set the teacups to cook in the oven, and when the eggs are just set and no more, press on them some more rice. Turn them out of the teacups, and if you have rubbed the inside of the cups with a little butter this will be easy, and sprinkle over the top of each mold plenty of chopped parsley. Do not forget salt and pepper to season the ingredients.

[*Pour la Patrie.*]

BROAD BEANS IN SAUCE

Take your shelled beans, very young and tender. Throw them into boiling water for a minute, then pour the water away. Heat for a pound of beans one and one-half pints of milk, stir in four ounces of salt butter, a very little chopped parsley, salt and pepper. Do not let the milk boil, but when it simmers put in the beans. When they have been heated for ten minutes, thicken your sauce with the yolks of two eggs and a tablespoonful of cream. Take out a bean and eat it to see if it is cooked, and if so, pour all on a hot dish. Garnish with fried sippets of bread. Old broad beans can be treated in the same way, but they must first be skinned.

[*Aimee.*]

OMELETTE OF PEAS

Beat up three eggs, to which add one tablespoonful of grated cheese, pepper, and salt, and mix thoroughly. Butter an omelette pan, and pour in the mixture, keep moving it gently with a fork while you sprinkle in with the other hand some cooked green peas. The omelette will be cooked by the time you have sprinkled in two handfuls. Slip it off on to a very hot dish, fold over, and serve at once.

[*Jean O.*]

BRUSSELS ARTICHOKES

Wash well some globe artichokes, and boil them in salted water. Meanwhile make a good mushroom filling, highly seasoned, of cooked mushroom, dipped into butter, pepper, salt, a few breadcrumbs, and shreds of ham. Remove the center leaves from the vegetable and as much of the choke as you can. Fill up with the mushroom force and stew gently in brown sauce flavored with a bunch of herbs.

[*F. R.*]

BELGIAN SALAD

is merely endive, washed and torn apart with red peppers added here and there as well as the ordinary salad dressing.

Belgian asparagus is done by adding to the cooked vegetable a bechamel sauce, poured over the dish, and then slices of hard boiled eggs placed on the top. The giant asparagus is used, and it is eaten with a fork.

[*A Grocer's Wife.*]

BRUSSELS CARROTS

Cut young carrots in small pieces, blanch them in salted water; melt some butter in a stew pan, add enough water and meat extract to make sufficient to cover the carrots, season with pepper, salt and a pinch of sugar and toss the carrots in this till they are tender. Then add the yolk of an egg and a tablespoonful of cream, holding the pan just off the fire with the left hand, while you stir with the right. When it is well mixed pour all out on a vegetable dish and sprinkle over with chopped parsley.

[*Amie reconnaissante.*]

CARROTS AND EGGS

Make the same preparation as above, for the sauce, with the same seasonings, but add a dust of nutmeg. Then add half a pint of white stock which will be enough for a small bunch of carrots; simmer them for fifteen minutes and then break in three whole eggs, taking care that they fall apart from each other. Let them cook till nearly set (for they will go on cooking in the hot sauce after you remove them from the fire) and serve at once. This is nearly as good if you use old carrots sliced, instead of the young ones.

[*M. Zoeben.*]

CUCUMBERS AND TOMATOES

Take two earthenware pots and put some tomatoes to stew in one, in water, pepper, and salt. Peel a cucumber, open it, remove the seeds and stuff it with any forcemeat that you have; but a white one is best. Let it cook gently in some brown stock, well covered over. When tender put the cucumber along the dish and tomatoes on each side. A puree of potatoes can surround them.

[*A. Fanderverde.*]

RED HARICOTS

Soak some white haricot-beans over night, or stew them till tender in some weak stock. Make a tomato sauce in a saucepan, and flavor it rather strongly with made mustard, stirring well, so that it is well incorporated. When the beans are tender, drain them from the liquor (keeping them hot) and reduce that to half its quantity. Put back the beans and add the tomato sauce, heat for a couple of minutes, and serve with three-cornered pieces of toast.

[*Elise et Jean.*]

POTATOES A LA BRABANCONNE

Boil some potatoes, rub them through a sieve, add pepper, salt, and a tablespoonful of cream to a pound of potatoes, rub through a tammy again. Chop a shallot, a spring or two of parsley and mix them in, sprinkling in at the same time a dust of nutmeg and a dessertspoonful of grated cheese. Place the puree in a dish to be baked, and before setting it in the oven sprinkle on the top some bread-crumbs, and cheese grated and mixed and one or two pats of salt butter. Bake till it is a golden brown.

[*Elise et Jean.*]

FLEMISH PEAS

Cook some young peas and some carrots (scraped and shaped into cones) in separate pans. Then put them together in an earthenware close covered pan to simmer together in butter and gravy, the first water having been well drained from them. Season with pepper and salt and let them cook gently for ten or twelve minutes; do not uncover the pot to stir it, but shake it every now and then to prevent the contents from burning.

[*Amie inconnue.*]

CHOU-CROUTE

Take as many white September cabbages as you wish, trim them, cut in halves, remove the stalks, wash them very thoroughly and shred them pretty finely. Procure an earthenware crock and put in a layer of cabbage, sprinkle it with coarse salt, whole pepper, and juniper berries. Fill up the crock in this way, put on the lid, and keep it down closely with weights. It will be ready in about six weeks' time, when the fermentation has taken place. It is good with pork or bacon.

SPINACH FRITTERS

Take any cold boiled spinach—though people generally eat all that there is—and mix it thickly with the yolk of egg and a little rice flour; you may add a little powdered sugar. Have ready some boiling fat, and drop spoonfuls of the spinach into it. If the fat is hot enough the fritters will puff out. Drain them quickly and serve very hot.

HARLEQUIN CABBAGES

Shred some red cabbage, to half a pound of it add two medium sized apples, minced finely without core or skin, a bit of fat bacon, season with pepper, salt, vinegar, which should be tarragon vinegar, and put it to simmer in some gravy or milk and water. It should cook for an hour over a gentle fire. Cook separately some green cabbage, cleaned, boiled till tender in salted water, chopped, then put back on a gentle fire with salt, pepper, a dust of nutmeg, and some fat or butter. Let it heat and mix well, and then serve the two colors side by side in the same dish; the red cabbage has a sour and the green has a nutty flavor which is very agreeable.

LITTLE TOWERS OF SALAD

Put a couple of eggs on to boil hard, while you make a thick mayonnaise sauce. Cut some beetroot, some cucumber, some cold potato, some tomato into slices. Peel your eggs, and slice them, and build up little piles of the different things, till about two inches high. Between each slice you will sprinkle grated breadcrumbs, pepper, salt, a tiny scrap of chopped raw shallot, parsley, all mixed in a cup. Finish with the rounded ends of white of egg on the top, put lettuce round and pour the dressing over it.

PUFFS FOR FRIDAY

Make a batter of a beaten egg, a dust of rice flour, pepper, salt and as much cream as you can give. Roll out this batter so thinly that you can almost see through it. Cut it into rounds and put on it any cooked vegetables that you have, but they must be highly seasoned. Cold potatoes will do if they are done with mustard, vinegar, or a strong boiled sauce. Fold over the paste, press it together at the edges, and fry in hot fat.

HADDOCK A LA CARDINAL

Take some fillets of haddock, or cod or hake, and poach them gently in milk and water. Meanwhile, prepare a good white sauce, and in another pan a thick tomato sauce, highly seasoned, colored with cochineal if need be, and as thick as a good cream. Lay the fillets when cooked one each on a plate, put some of the white sauce round it, and along the top put the tomato sauce which must not run down. A sprig of chervil is to be placed at each end of the fillet.

[*Seulette.*]

SKATE STEW

Put the fins, skin, trimmings of skate into water enough to cook them, with pepper and salt and simmer for half an hour. Strain it through a fine sieve. Make a brown sauce of butter and flour, pepper, salt, adding a little milk, about a teacupful for a pound of skate, then squeeze in the juice of half a lemon, and if you have it, a glass of white wine. Take the skate, cut it in pieces, simmer it in salted water; when cooked, strain away the water, dish the fish, pouring over it the above sauce. Decorate with strips of lemon peel laid in a lattice-work down the center.

[*Une epiciere.*]

TO DRESS COARSE FISH

Any fish is good if dressed in this way. Make a brown sauce, well flouring it with salt, pepper, and dried herbs. Mince and fry a shallot and add it, then a large glass of red wine, a few drops of lemon juice. Cook some fish roe, sieve it, and stir it into the sauce. Take your fish and simmer it in milk and water till cooked, then heat it up quickly in the sauce to serve.

[*F. R.*]

FLEMISH SALAD

This is fillets of herring, laid in a bowl with slices of apple, beetroot, cold potatoes, and cold cooked sprouts, covered with the ordinary salad dressing. If the fish is salted, let it soak first of all in milk to take away the greater part of the salt. This is a winter dish, but the same sort of thing is prepared in summer, substituting cold cooked peas, cauliflower, artichokes, beans, with the fish.

[*Amie reconnaissante.*]

FLEMISH SAUCE

This popular sauce is composed of melted butter thickened with yolk of egg and flavored with mustard; it is used greatly for fish.

BEEF SQUARES

If you have a small piece of very good beef, such as rump steak or fillet of beef, it is more economical to cut it into squares, and grill it lightly at a clear fire. Have ready some squares of toast, buttered and hot, lay these on a hot dish with a bit of steak on the top, and on the top of that a slice of tomato much peppered and salted and a small pile of horse-radish. This makes a pretty dish and can be varied by using capers or chopped gherkins instead of horse-radish. It is a great saving to cut meat, bread, etc., in squares instead of rounds.

[*Une amie au convent.*]

IMITATION CUTLETS

A dish that I have done for those who like curry flavoring is the following. Take any cold cooked vegetables, and cutting them in small pieces, roll them in a thick white sauce which you have strongly flavored with curry. Put it aside to get firm. If you are in a hurry you can bind with the yolk of an egg in the flour and make a thick batter in that way. Form into cutlets and fry as you would a real cutlet. The same thing can be done with macaroni or spaghetti that is already cooked, with cold fish or anything that is insipid to the taste.

[*Une amie au convent.*]

KIDNEYS WITH MADEIRA

Use either sheep or pigs' kidneys. Cut them longways, so as to be able to take out the threads from the inside of them. Put some butter on to fry over a brisk fire and when it is browned, but not burnt, put in the kidneys for three or four minutes. Take them out and keep them hot for a minute while you add to the butter they were cooked in a soupspoonful of Madeira wine, a good dust of chopped parsley, a little cayenne pepper and salt. Mix it well, and if too thick add a little gravy. Pour the sauce over the kidneys and finish with a powdering of chopped parsley. Fried potatoes are eaten with this dish.

[*Mme. Vanderbelle Genotte.*]

PIGS' TROTTERS IN BLANQUETTE

Any part of pork or veal is good done in this way. Take your pieces of meat and fry them in butter till they are a good golden brown color. Put them in a pan, covering them with water, and adding a sliced onion, a bay leaf, a whole carrot, a leek, pepper, salt, —let it all simmer gently over a slow fire till the meat is cooked but not boiled. Take the pieces from the liquor and pass it through a sieve. Mix a little rice flour in a cup of cold water, stirring well. Drop in the juice of half a lemon and the beaten yolk of an egg, which stir round quickly. Put in the meat again for a moment and serve it with boiled potatoes.

LOIN OF MUTTON IN THE POT

Put in an earthenware pot three shallots, finely minced; take a bit of garlic, cut it close and rub it round the side of the pot; put in as well a lump of butter, pepper and salt, and some rather fat gravy. Divide the loin and put six chops in to simmer for three quarters of an hour on a moderate fire, covering the pot with the lid. Before you serve it, stir in a little lemon juice and stir up the sauce. To be served with Cauliflower à la Aerschot as follows: Cut your cauliflower into medium pieces, seeing that it is very clean, while you have some salted water boiling up. Put in the pieces, boil till tender, then drain them on a sieve. Put leaves and trimming of the vegetable into the pot to simmer and serve as basis for a vegetable soup. Make a good white sauce, adding the yolk of an egg, and flavoring it with nutmeg. Put the vegetable on a dish and pour over the sauce, letting it stand for a few moments by the fire before it is eaten.

[*Madame Herman Noppen.*]

OX TONGUE WITH SPINACH AND WHITE SAUCE

Boil the tongue in salted water till the outer skin will peel off. Take this off, then put the tongue back in the liquor to simmer while you prepare the same. Take a piece of butter the size of an egg, melt it and mix it with two dessertspoonfuls of ground rice, add some of the liquor, pepper, and salt, stir well, so that it makes a good cream; drop in the yolks of two eggs, always stirring, and a little lemon juice. Serve the tongue whole with this sauce poured over it and spinach done in the following way: Wash the spinach in running water till every bit of grit has gone. Put some water on to boil, salt it well, and throw in the spinach which you have freed from mid-rib and stalk. The water must be boiling and the fire brisk. When tender, pass the spinach through the sieve, then put a bit of butter into an enameled saucepan, then the spinach, which heat for six minutes, add a little pepper. Serve it with the tongue, and you can garnish as well with little croutons of bread fried in butter.

[*Madame Herman Noppen.*]

VEAL FRITTERS

If you have only a little piece of veal or other cold meat, you can make a very presentable dish in the following way: Cut a thin slice of meat and spread on each side of it a layer of mashed potatoes to which you have added some tomato sauce. Beat up an egg and dip the slices and potato into it, lay them in fine breadcrumbs and fry them till a good golden color in plenty of fat. Send them to table under a hot cover.

[*Pour la Patrie.*]

STEWED BEEF

If you are obliged to make a hot dish in a hurry and have only a piece of inferior meat, there is no better way of using it than by dressing it in the Brabant way, which is rather expensive. Clean and cook some mushrooms, and when fried lightly, add them and their liquor to your beef, cut up in small pieces, but not minced. Add pepper, salt, a dust of spices, or an onion with three or four cloves in it, and a half bottle of good red wine. Stew all together for at least twenty minutes, take out the onion and cloves, and serve in the dish it was cooked in which should be an earthenware pot.

[*Pour la Patrie.*]

A MUTTON SALAD

Cut some slices of cold mutton or lamb, removing every bit of fat and skin that you can, unless that destroys the firmness of the slice. Prepare a salad of lettuce, and if you cannot give a mayonnaise sauce, add to the lettuce plenty of sliced cucumber, for that keeps the mutton moist. Put the salad on each slice and roll the meat over as tightly as you can. Lay the rolls closely together in a dish and sprinkle a very little salad dressing over them. This way of doing meat is very useful for taking to picnics, or for taking on a long journey.

[*Pour la Patrie.*]

SAUSAGE PATTIES

Half a pound of sausage meat of any kind that you like. Make some rounds of paste, lay the meat on half of each round and fold over. Steam for quarter of an hour, or stew in plenty of gravy.

[*Pour la Patrie.*]

SAUSAGE AND POTATOES

Roll some cooked sausage meat in mashed potatoes, making a roll for each person. Brush the potatoes over with milk and put them to bake till nicely browned. Decorate with gherkins on each roll of butter.

[*Pour la Patrie.*]

RAGOUT OF COLD MEAT

Take any cold meat that you have, free it from fat and skin and cut it in rounds like a five-franc piece. If you have some lean bacon or ham, a little of that should be added. I should tell you first of all to put some rice on to boil in boiling water. Make a sauce of flour and butter in a pan, adding gravy if you happen to have it, but failing that, use water and vinegar in equal parts to thin it; season with pepper and salt and a small spoonful of anchovy sauce. When the sauce is heating, put in the meat and cover the pan, let it all heat for twelve minutes and then place meat and sauce in the middle of a dish. By this time the rice may be tender. Drain it well and put it as a border to the stew.

[*Aimee.*]

A QUICKLY MADE STEW

Put a piece of butter in a stewpan, with an onion cut in pieces, a few cloves, salt and pepper, a tablespoonful of shredded parsley, and if you have it some good gravy or meat juice and water. Throw into the sauce some cold meat, preferably underdone, and after it has simmered for fifteen minutes take a cut onion and rub with it the bottom of the dish that you are going to use. Take a good glass of red wine, such as Burgundy and mix it with the yolk of an egg, stir this into the stew and serve up in a couple of minutes.

[*Madame Groubet.*]

GRENADINES OF VEAL

Take a fireproof dish, and after sprinkling it with breadcrumbs put in it a layer of roast veal in slices, a layer of mashed potatoes, a layer of veal kidney, partly cooked, and cut into pieces and lastly a layer of potato. Cover the whole with a bechamel sauce into which you have stirred some grated cheese; put it to bake in the oven. Then make a brown sauce with any veal or kidney gravy that you have, and cook some mushrooms in it with pepper and salt; the sauce is to be served with the grenadine.

HOCHE POT

Slice an onion and fry it in butter till it is brown; add pieces of pork and of mutton freed from fat and skin; cover them with water and throw into it any kinds of vegetables that you may have; but particularly sliced carrots and turnips and green cabbages; put it in the oven to cook. In another saucepan boil some white haricot beans, salt, and pepper, until they are tender, when they must be added to the stew with a small quantity of the liquor that they have been boiled in.

PIGEON AND CABBAGE ROLLS

Take two pigeons, two cabbages, four slices of fried bacon, an ounce of butter, a large wineglassful of sherry, and some gravy. Truss your pigeons and cook them in butter for ten minutes in a fireproof dish. Then take them out, cut them into neat pieces. Meanwhile have the cabbages boiled in salted water. Drain them. Cut them in small pieces and roll some up in each slice of bacon; lay the pigeons on top, pouring over them the liquor they were cooked in and half the wine. Put all in the oven for ten minutes—pour in the rest of the wine and leave for another ten minutes before serving. If you have stock to add to this it is an improvement, or put half a teaspoonful of meat extract to half a pint of water.

[*Une refugiee.*]

REMAINS OF SAUSAGE

If you have a few inches of a big sausage cut it into as thick slices as you can—fry them and lay them in a circle on a dish with a poached egg on each. Little dinner breads are good when soaked in milk, stuffed with sausage meat, and fried. It can be used to stuff cucumber, or eggplants, but you should then crumble up the meat and bind it with the yolk of a raw egg.

[*Mme. Georgette.*]

SHOULDER OF LAMB A LA BEIGE

Braise your shoulder of lamb; that is, put it in a closely covered stewpan, in a good brown sauce or gravy with the vegetables, to be served with it. It is the lid being closed that makes the meat take some flavor from the vegetables. To do it in the Belgian way, take some good white turnips, wash them and scrape them, put small ones in whole, large ones cut in half. Take some small cabbages, trim off without leaves, cut them in half, remove the stalk, make a hollow in the center and fill it with forcemeat of any kind; but sausage meat is good. Place the stuffed cabbages round the meat to cook gently at the same time.

[*Madame Vershagen.*]

FILLET OF BEEF À LA BRABANCONNE

Take a whole fillet of beef, trim it neatly and set it in a braising pan to cook very slowly in some good brown sauce to which you have added a pint of stock. Put in neatly shaped carrots and turnips and some balls made of mashed potato already fried. Keep hot in two sauceboats a puree of Brussels sprouts and a puree of onions. These are prepared by cooking the vegetables in water, then chopping fine, and rubbing through a sieve with cream, or with a little good milk, pepper, and salt. To serve the fillet, lay it on a dish with the carrots and turnip, potato cakes round; pour over it the rest of the brown sauce from the pan; then add in heaps the onion puree and the sprouts puree.

[*Madame Vershagen.*]

STEWED BEEF

An inferior part of beef may be made to taste excellent if it is braised; that is, simmered with the cover on slowly, in company with onions (already fried) and well washed pieces of carrots and whole turnips. Put on also some small cabbages cut in halves, and if you can give it, a glass of good red wine.

[*Une refugiee.*]

BEEF AND APRICOTS

Stew your beef, say three pounds of steak, in some gravy, adding to a pint of liquor a level teaspoonful of white sugar. Throw in a handful of the dried apricots, but be sure you wash them well first. This dish is generally accompanied by leeks, first blanched for a few moments, and then put in the stew. Flavor with salt, pepper, and the rind of half a lemon which remove before you serve the stew. For English taste the sugar could be omitted.

[*Seulette.*]

FOR AN INVALID

This must be begun at least three hours before it will be required. Take two ounces of pearl barley, wash it well, and put it in cold water enough to cover it, for an hour. Take a pound of good steak, shred it in small pieces, and put it in an enameled saucepan with a quart of cold water and a sprinkle of salt. Strain the water from the barley and add this last to the meat, and let it simmer for two hours. Then strain off the liquor and pound the meat and barley in a mortar, rub it through a sieve; when it is a smooth puree put it back into the pan with its liquor and a gill of cream. Let it simmer again for a moment and serve it in a cup with a lid to it.

[*Madame A. F.*]

INVALIDS' EGGS

Cut out some rounds of bread a good deal larger than a poached egg would be. While these are frying, make a puree of Brussels sprouts. Boil them till tender, squeeze in a cloth. Rub them through a sieve and make into a very thick puree with cream, pepper and salt. Poach a fresh egg for each crouton, and slip it on, very quickly, put some of the green puree round, and serve under a hot cover.

A SWEET FOR THE CHILDREN

If you have some little breads over, cut each one in four, soak the pieces in milk sweetened and flavored with vanilla, for three hours. When they are well soaked roll them for a moment in grated and dried breadcrumbs, and dip them for a moment in boiling fat, just as you would do croquettes. Sift some white sugar over them and serve very hot.

[*Madame M.*]

QUINCE CUSTARD

When you have quince preserves by you this is a quickly prepared dish. Make a good custard with a pint of rich milk, four eggs and a little essence of almonds and two ounces of powdered sugar. Put your quince preserve at the bottom of a fireproof circular dish and fill up with custard. Put it to bake for half or hour or till set. When set add some more quince (heated) on the top with some chopped almonds and serve hot. The same dish can be done with apples, which should be stewed, flavored with the rind of a half lemon, and passed through a sieve. Apple puree is put on the top in the same way, and it is decorated with some thin lemon peel cut into stars.

[*Chef reconnaissant.*]

YELLOW PLUMS AND RICE

Put half a pound of rice in hot milk till it has absorbed all it can and is tender. Beat lightly the yolks of three eggs, beating in a lump of fresh butter the size of a pullet's egg; add powdered sugar and the whites of the eggs well beaten. Put the rice into this mixture and place all in a mold. Cook it gently for twenty-five minutes. Meanwhile take some very perfect yellow plums, skin and stone them and heat them in half a bottle of light white wine that you have seasoned with a little spice. Turn out the rice, put the yellow plums on the top and pour round the sauce, strained through muslin. Very good cold.

BRABANT PANCAKE

Butter first of all your pancakes, and you should have proper pancake saucers fit to go to table. Heat half a pint of sweetened milk and melt a quarter of a pound of salt butter with it. When well melted pour it into a basin and sprinkle in nearly three ounces of flour. Beat up the yolks of three large or four small eggs and incorporate them, then add the whites well beaten. Put a spoonful or two on each saucer and set to bake in the oven for ten minutes and when done place each saucer on a plate with a good lump of apricot jam on each. If you have no pancake saucers, put the apricot preserve on one half of each pancake and fold it up.

[*Jean O.*]

DELICIOUS SAUCE FOR PUDDINGS

To a large wineglassful (say a glass for champagne wine) of new Madeira add the yolks only of two eggs. Put in a very clean enamel saucepan over the fire and stir in powdered sugar to your taste. Whisk it over the fire till it froths, but do not allow it even to simmer. Use for Genoese cakes and puddings.

[*Madame Groubet.*]

FRUIT JELLIES

Jellies that are very well flavored can be made with fresh fruit, raspberries, strawberries, apricots, or even rhubarb, using the proportions of one ounce of gelatine (in cold weather) to every pound of fruit puree. In hot weather use a little less gelatine. As the fruit generally gives a bad color, you must use cochineal for the red jellies and a little green coloring for gooseberry jellies. The gelatine is of course melted in the fruit puree and all turned into a mold. You can make your own green coloring in this way. Pick a pound of spinach, throwing away the stalks and midrib. Put it on in a pan with a little salt and keep the cover down. Let it boil for twelve minutes. Then put a fine sieve over a basin and pour the spinach water through it. Strain the spinach water once or twice through muslin; it will be a good color and will keep some time. Orange and lemon jellies are much more wholesome when made at home than those made from bought powders. To the juice of every six oranges you should add the juice of one lemon, and you will procure twice as much juice from the fruit if, just before you squeeze it, you let it soak in hot water for three or four minutes.

[*Pour la Patrie.*]

STRAWBERRY FANCY

Take a slice or two of plain sponge cake and cut out rounds two inches across. Then whip up in a basin the whites only of four eggs, coloring them with the thinner part of strawberry jam. As a rule this jam is not red enough, and you must add a little cochineal. Put the pink mixture in high piles on the cakes.

[*Pour la Patrie.*]

PINK RICE

This sweet is liked by children who are tired of rice pudding. Boil your rice and when tender mix in with it the juice of a boiled beetroot to which some sugar has been added. Turn it into a mold and when cold remove it and serve it with a spoonful of raspberry preserve on the top or with some red plums round it.

[*Pour la Patrie.*]

MILITARY PRUNES

Take some of the best French preserved prunes, and remove the stones. Soak them in orange curaçoa for as long a time as you have at your disposal. Then replace each stone by a blanched almond, and place the prunes in small crystal dishes.

[*Pour la Patrie.*]

MADELINE CHERRIES

Take some Madeleine cakes and scoop them out to form baskets. Fill these with stoned cherries both white and black that you have soaked in a good liqueur—cherry brandy is the best but you may use maraschino. Place two long strips of angelica across the top and where these intersect a very fine stoned cherry.

[*Pour la Patrie.*]

STRAWBERRY TARTLETS

It often happens that you have among the strawberries a quantity that are not quite good enough to be sent to table as dessert, and yet not enough to make jam of. Put these strawberries on to heat, with some brown sugar, and use them to fill small pastry tartlets. Pastry cases can be bought for very little at the confectioner's. Cover the top of the tartlet when the strawberry conserve is cold with whipped cream.

[*Pour la Patrie.*]

MADEIRA EGGS OR OEUFS À LA GRAND'MÈRE

Break the yolk of an egg in a basin and be sure that it is very fresh; beat it up, adding a little powdered sugar, and then, drop by drop, enough of the best Madeira to give it a strong flavor. This makes a nice sweet served in glass cups and it is besides very good for sore throats.

[*Pour la Patrie.*]

BUTTERFLIES

You will get at the confectioner's small round cakes that are smooth on the top; they are plain, and are about two and one-half inches across. Take one and cut it in halves, separating the top from the bottom. Cut the top pieces right across; you have now two half moons. Put some honey along the one straight edge of each half moon and stick it by that on the lower piece of cake, a little to one side. Do the same with the second half moon, so that they both stick up, not unlike wings. Fill the space between with a thick mixture of chopped almonds rolled in honey, and place two strips of angelica poking forward to suggest antennae. A good nougat will answer instead of the honey.

[*Pour la Patrie.*]

CHERRY AND STRAWBERRY COMPOTE

Take half a pint of rich cream and mix with it a small glassful of Madeira wine or of good brandy. Pick over some fine cherries and strawberries, stoning the cherries, and taking out the little center piece of each strawberry that is attached to the stalk. Lay your fruit in a shallow dish and cover it with the liquor and serve with the long sponge biscuits known as "langues de chat" (Savoy fingers).

[*Amitie aux Anglais.*]

CHOCOLATE CUSTARD

To make a nice sweet in a few minutes can be easily managed if you follow this recipe. Make a custard of rich milk and yolks of eggs, sweeten it with sugar, flavored with vanilla, and if you have a little cream add that also. Then grate down some of the best chocolate, as finely as you can, rub it through coarse muslin so that it is a fine powder. Stir this with your custard, always stirring one way so that no bubbles of air get in. When you have got a thick consistency like rich cream, pour the mixture into paper or china cases, sprinkle over the tops with chopped almonds. There is no cooking required.

GOOSEBERRY CREAM WITHOUT CREAM

Take your gooseberries and wash them well, cut off the stalk and the black tip of each. Stew them with sugar till they are tender, just covered in water. Do not let them burn. If you have not time to attend to that put them in the oven in a shallow dish sprinkled with brown sugar. When tender rub them through a fine sieve at least twice. Flavor with a few drops of lemon juice, and add sugar if required. Then beat up a fresh egg in milk and add as much arrowroot or cornflour as will lie flat in a salt spoon. Mix the custard with the gooseberries, pass it through the sieve once more and serve it in a crystal bowl.

[*Mdlle. B-M.*]

CHOCOLATE PUDDINGS

Make some Genoese cake mixture as you would for a light cake, and pour it into greased molds like cups. You can take the weight of one egg in dried flour, butter, and rather less of sugar. Beat the butter and sugar together to a cream, sprinkle in the flour, stirring all the time, a pinch of salt, and then the beaten egg. When your little cakes are baked, turn them out of the molds and when cool turn them upside down and remove the inside, leaving a deep hole and a thin crust all round. Fill up this hole with the custard and chocolate as above, and let it grow firm. Then turn the cases right way up and pour over the top a sweet cherry sauce. You may require the yolks of two eggs to make the custard firm.

[*Mdlle. B-M.*]

6458590R00056

Printed in Great Britain
by Amazon.co.uk, Ltd.,
Marston Gate.